THE SPHINX AND HER CIRCLE

By the same author

★

MADAME DE GENLIS

Ada Leverson

VIOLET WYNDHAM

The Sphinx and Her Circle

a biographical sketch of
Ada Leverson
1862-1933

NEW YORK
THE VANGUARD PRESS, INC.

Library of Congress Card Catalogue Number: 64-16261

To
Osbert Sitwell

The subject of this sketch had the writer's gift of being able to describe people and events verbally and in so vivid a manner that they became engraved upon the hearer's imagination. For this reason I feel that I knew people who died before I was born, or lived and died at a time when I was too young to take them in. With the help of what she and her contemporaries have told me; of letters, and extracts from her novels, which I know to have been derived from life; of her other works that reveal her true self; and of my own memories, I have attempted to write this short biographical study of my mother. Of the twenty-nine or so letters and telegrams extant that were written to her by Oscar Wilde, I have included only a few, as all of them have been published in *The Letters of Oscar Wilde*, edited by Rupert Hart-Davis.

*To the Sphinx of Pleasure from
the Singer of Pain*

Dedication by Oscar Wilde
in Ada Leverson's copy of
The Ballad of Reading Gaol,
1899

ILLUSTRATIONS

*The portrait of Prince Henri d'Orléans is reproduced by courtesy
of the Bibliotheque Nationale, Paris; that of W. Somerset
Maugham by courtesy of the artist; that of Oscar Wilde by
courtesy of the Gernsheim Collection; and that of Mrs Cyril
Martineau by courtesy of Mr Henry Vyner.*

I am grateful to Sir Osbert Sitwell for giving his permission to publish his letters, also to Mr T. S. Eliot and to Mr Harold Acton for permission to publish theirs; to Mr Edward W. Colman, Mr C. D. Medley and Sir John Rothenstein for permission to publish respectively the letters of Lord Alfred Douglas, George Moore and William Rothenstein; to Mr J. P. Ross for permission to publish the letters of Robert Ross; and to Myrtle R. Butcher and Harold J. Dies, trustees of the Dreiser Trust, for permission to publish a letter from Theodore Dreiser.

CHAPTER I

Ada Leverson had a retiring nature. She believed in her talent, which she hoped would be recognised, but the thought of personal publicity horrified her. It is, therefore, ironic that her name is known more for having been associated with the principal character in a world-wide scandal than as a writer: it was she and her husband who gave Oscar Wilde shelter between his trials. Her six novels, first published between 1907 and 1916, were well received by reviewers and gained many devotees but it was not until 1960 that their high literary quality began to be fully recognised. This recognition has been accompanied by a growing curiosity about her life which it is hoped the following study may help to satisfy.

Ada Leverson's back-ground is not an easy one to classify; so many different elements are contained in it. A recorded pedigree exists on her maternal grandfather's side, which goes back to the late sixteenth century, when Don Cesar Orobio was born in Braganza. He was a Marrano Jew and was burnt at the stake in Seville for refusing to abandon the Jewish faith. His son, Don Balthazar (Isaac) Orobio de Castro,* although a remote ancestor – he was born in 1620 – is of interest in a study of Ada because he bequeathed to his descendants a high standard of integrity. After witnessing the martyrdom of his father and suffering three years'

---

* *The Dramatic Life of Orobio De Castro* by Augusto D'Esaguy, reprinted from Bulletin of the Institute of the History of Medicine, Vol. v, No. 9, November, 1937.
History of the Marranos by Cecil Roth, Routledge, 1933.

imprisonment in the dungeons of Seville, he left Spain for France. There, by reason of his former high reputation in Spain, he was appointed physician and privy councillor to Louis xiv. It was then that the nobility of his character revealed itself. Unable to forget that he was the son of a martyr, he could not live with peace of mind in a country where the faith for which his father had died could not be practised openly. He obeyed the call of his conscience, renounced his honours in France and went to live in Amsterdam, where his house became the centre of the city's intellectual life. He wrote many works in Latin, in one of which he opposed the views of his friend Spinoza. Several historians and scholars have dealt with his life and works. One of his descendants, Rebecca Orobio Furtado, married Isaac Simon in Jamaica in 1816. Isaac's mother had been born Caroline Taylor; her brother, Major-General Sir Thomas Taylor, was captivated by the beauty of his nephew Isaac as a child and wished to adopt him as his heir, but his parents would not part with him. The Taylors were a Wiltshire family who owned property in Jamaica.

The Simons and the Orobios had owned land in Jamaica since 1740, when the act was passed in England naturalising Jews. Isaac Simon took an active part in the emancipation of slaves in Jamaica and is reputed to have been the first slave-owner there to liberate his own; he protected the missionaries, many of whom would have lost their lives in the insurrections of 1830 and 1831 but for his influence. John Simon, Isaac's son and Ada's grandfather, was Liberal Member for Dewsbury for twenty years and received a knighthood. He was a typical high-minded Victorian: his wife, Rachel, was reflective and demonstrably affectionate. The Simons were living in Tavistock Square when their daughter Zillah married Samuel Henry Beddington, whose father had made a fortune in wool, bringing it in his own ships to England from Australia. This fortune was invested in property in and near London including Beddington from which the family took its name. Samuel and Zillah were Ada's father and mother.

The character of Mr Woodhouse in Jane Austen's *Emma* might have been a portrait of Ada's father. Nervous about his health and the health of others, he would not allow his children to touch money, in case it carried germs. He ate only roast chicken, fried sole, boiled salmon, or apple tart, and drank only white wine, barley water or tea. He disliked ostentation, but lived in comfort, at 21 Hyde Park Square, served by a butler called Leggatt, a red-faced coachman called Eades, and, among other servants, a housemaid called Elizabeth, whose chief duty was to bring her master a cup of tea at five o'clock in the morning. He was one of the first to abandon the horse carriage in favour of an electric brougham, in the front of which Eades and a footman would sit, perched perilously over nothing.

Zillah became one of the best amateur pianists of her day. Perhaps this gift may have been inherited from a great-grandmother, Rachel Samuel, who had been a pupil of Dr Burney. An English harpsichord, made by Jacob Kirkman, chosen by Burney for his pupil, was a treasured possession of the family until not very long ago, when it was presented to the Victoria and Albert Museum.

We see in Ada's heredity a love of erudition, steadfastness, musical talent and business ability. Of the latter she was completely devoid; her musical talent was slight; of her love of erudition and her steadfastness there is no doubt.

Zillah took little interest in her four sons, admired her four daughters, but only really cared for playing the piano and listening to the best musicians of her day, most of whom sooner or later visited Hyde Park Square. She had a sweet simplicity about her and appeared unconscious of

what was going on beneath the surface; yet she would
have flashes of insight, known in her family as 'Mamma's
flashlights'.

As Ada grew up she drew away from her mother's world
of music; her interest was in books. Observing this, her
father engaged a graduate of Girton to teach her the classics.
Having been well grounded earlier in French and German,
a wide field of literature lay open to her. This education was
the foundation of her literary style.

Ada would say in later years that she learned much about
human nature in the nursery and the schoolroom. As an
example, she would tell how one of her brothers, when he was
a tiny child, would urge her to help him tie two chairs
together and pretend they were a carriage; yet when taken
in a real one he showed no interest at all in the outing.
This, Ada maintained, showed a preference for make-
believe to reality as revealed in the adult's love of the theatre.

Evelyn, the second daughter, had a sweet nature and
several other attributes which inspired romantic passions
and caused dramas. She had brown eyes, golden hair, a
beautiful singing voice and an air of mystery. She and her
elder sister were close friends in the schoolroom, and when
the time came for them to attend their first dances, they
would drive together, hearts beating fast with excitement,
while Ada, always too pale, would rub her face to make it
pink, and Evelyn would hang her head out of the carriage
window to cool her glowing cheeks.

The third daughter, Sybil, had an affectionate nature, a
piquant prettiness and a pertness about her manner which
charmed her father. Violet, the youngest of the family,
known by them all as 'Babs', had a calm, quiet nature, great
intelligence and innate goodness, all of which combined to
make her the confidante of her brothers and sisters from the
early age of ten. As she grew up she achieved a great

Mrs Beddington, Ada Leverson's mother

From a painting by Sir John Millais, PRA

Sybil Seligman

From a drawing by Helleu

Violet Schiff

serenity and felt secure in her knowledge that she was extremely pretty and her father's favourite child.

Of the four sons, George, the eldest, was the flower of the flock. He was handsome, witty and intelligent, and Ada's favourite of her brothers and sisters. He died of typhoid fever at the age of twenty-one. Then came Charles, who became a barrister, was to adore his wife and sons, and would always be ready to listen to, or to make a joke. Frank, of whom his sisters were always fond, was a soldier and an athlete. Arthur, the youngest son, died young.

The Beddington girls, well brought-up and well dowered, were much sought in marriage. Both Ada and Sybil married against their father's wishes in their anxiety to gain freedom from parental control.

Ernest Leverson proposed marriage when Ada was nineteen and was accepted at once. He was twelve years older than she, and possessed the charm of experience. After the marriage it was a shock to discover that a little girl being brought up in a convent in Paris, whom he had described as his ward, was in reality his illegitimate daughter. Ada and Ernest were to have two children; a son who died in early childhood, and later, a daughter.

Ernest was the son of George Leverson, a prosperous diamond merchant of the second generation. His first wife, Henrietta Johnasson, had lived with her family in a country house near Durham. She gave her husband several sons who all idolized her. After her death in the Nineties, George Leverson re-married; this time he chose the grey-haired daughter of a dignitary of the Church of England. The character of Aunt William in Ada's novel *The Twelfth Hour*, described as being 'one of those rare women of theory rather than practice who preferred a menu to a dinner and a recipe to either,' was taken from Henrietta. Lady Kellynch, in the novel *Bird of Paradise*, is a composite portrait drawn

by Ada of her mother-in-law and her step-mother-in-law.
This is how she is described:

' "Percy will soon be home, I suppose? Today is the day
he goes to the Queen's Hall, isn't it?" asked Lady Kellynch
who thought any Hall was highly honoured by Percy's
presence and lucky to get it. She really knew hardly anyone
by sight except her sons and this was the more odd as she
had a particularly large circle of acquaintance and made a
point of accepting and returning every invitation she received,
invariably being amongst those present at every possible
form of entertainment and punctiliously calling on people
afterwards. She was always mounting staircases, going up
in lifts, and driving about leaving cards. Bertha always
wondered at her gregariousness since one would fancy she
could have got very little satisfaction with a crowd of people
whom she forgot the instant they were out of sight.'

George Leverson was a sybarite who insisted on good
cooking and a well-run house. He was known to have thrown
a badly-roasted joint at a footman, a gesture which has been
attributed with pride to so many that it has become a cliché.
It was a period when a violent temper in a man was respected.
Other interests of his were Garibaldi, whom he knew
personally, and European travel. His death occurred suddenly
on a platform at Victoria Station, an incident which should
serve as a warning to those who feel too deeply a shortage of
porters, the loss of luggage, or the missing of a train.
George Leverson believed that Jews who were lucky enough
to be born in England should intermarry and thereby be
assimilated.

Ernest worked in the City, to which he was driven daily
in a private hansom from his house in Courtfield Gardens.
His brothers, George and Julian, both went to Woolwich
and ultimately became colonels in the Royal Engineers.
George married the daughter of a country clergyman.

Julian, after spending many years in India, returned to England to enjoy a full social life as a bachelor. Kind, dependable and fair-minded, he was always close to Ada and the most stable member of her and her husband's family.

Soon after her marriage, an estrangement began between Ada and her sister Evelyn, the exact reason for which has never been known. It is probable that mischief of some kind had been made by the German governess who had educated the boys until public-school age and had been the mentor of the girls until they grew up. Later Ada saw a resemblance in her to a character in a Balzac novel, perhaps to Cousine Bette. Making trouble between the sisters was not enough for the governess; she introduced her pretty niece Nelly to the family, who became admired too much by Evelyn's husband, causing sorrow and blunders which ended in the untimely death of the young husband.

Mr Beddington would make hasty decisions (they were generally right) which he would never revoke. He forbade any of his family to speak to the governess again. Ada considered this edict unjust and continued to be her friend; in her view the troubles were accidental and she refused to forego the loyalty she felt towards someone she had respected since childhood. No one dared tell her father that Ada was disobeying him. In this action there began an estrangement with Evelyn and a slight gulf between Ada and her other sisters.

Marguerite Leverson, Ernest's first cousin, married Brandon Thomas, the author of *Charley's Aunt*. The play was almost a family affair, as the name 'Charley' was taken from that of Ada's brother. The two young couples saw a lot of each other in the late Eighties and laughter was very much in the air. It was in theatres, music-halls and books,

and brought to the drawing-room by a brilliant entertainer
called Corney Grain. Ada's outlook and her work were
influenced by the humour of her time. She grew up with
Francis Burnand's *Happy Thoughts,* and later Weedon
Grossmith's *Diary of a Nobody.*

Corney Grain's wit helped in the development of Ada's
sense of satire. He died in 1895, and his name is almost
forgotten. It is difficult to envisage the cause of his enormous
popularity. Tall, large and handsome, he was also extremely
gentlemanly. As a young man he had been called to the bar,
but in 1870 abandoned a legal career to join the German
Reed Entertainment Company. Soon he became an inde-
pendent entertainer, singing satirical lyrics to his own
accompaniment at the piano. He had a biting wit, always
free from innuendo, which convulsed his audiences. Once,
when Ada and Ernest had engaged him to entertain at a
party, he arrived a little late. His first number was a parody
of a certain popular Italian song, and the manner in which the
composer sang it. It happened that the composer had just
sung it before Corney Grain arrived. No one knew whether to
laugh; however the composer, Paolo Tosti, had a wit of his
own and the tact of a diplomat. The mistake was carried off
by him so well that the audience ended by believing the
affair had been premeditated.

This was the light side of Ada's life which, alas, concealed
a certain melancholy. She had made the discovery that she
was never to know the happiness of living with someone with
whom she was in love; that the rest of her life would have to
be a compromise. The episode which had brought home this
sad fact to Ada had occurred in Monte Carlo where Ernest
had displayed the shallowness of his interest in her by spending all afternoons and most nights at the Casino. To
be left quite alone in a place whose very name is a symbol of
pleasure would have been a depressing experience for any

lively young woman. Ernest's friends shared his love of gambling; there was no one whose companionship she could enjoy. As it dawned upon Ada that her marriage had been a mistake, she became overwhelmed with loneliness. It was in this vulnerable mood that William, 4th Earl of Desart, a handsome man and a poet, was introduced to her. He had stepped off a beautiful yacht, also unhappy and in need of consolation. They fell in love. That he was a good deal older than Ada did not detract from his charm for her. Ernest saw no harm in his wife sailing away on a week's cruise with another man. He preferred to remain near the Casino. Lady Desart had recently left her husband for an actor called Sugden. The divorce which ensued had created a sensation. Was Lord Desart free when he fell in love with Ada? Or had he found his second marriage a disappointment? The date of their meeting is not known. She was obliged to renounce this romantic attachment because, although she was no longer in love with her husband, she dreaded causing him unhappiness.

Light is thrown upon Ada's thoughts at the start of her literary career in some letters of hers written in 1891 to George Moore who was then thirty-nine. These were found more than fifty years after they were written, in a drawer of a mahogany escritoire which had belonged to George Moore's great friend, Lady Cunard, and had been bought at a sale of her furniture. It is ironic that most of the letters contain the words 'Please destroy this,' and it is obvious on reading them that vanity was the cause of Moore's failure to accede to the request: 'There is something very peculiarly attractive about you, your talent, your intellect, your original way of looking at things, and your wayward-ness is also a singular charm to me,' Ada writes in one of them.

In another she tells him: 'On Saturday I wrote a sort of

little sketch which I have sent to the publishers. It is sure to
be returned of course, and then I will send it to you and you
must tell me whether you think it very stupid.' A few days
later: 'I am most delighted at what you say. I quite see
what you mean. I can alter the third chapter.' Then: 'I
send you the little story with the third chapter re-written.
I do hope you will like it better. Tell me what you think of
it.' Again: 'You cannot imagine how anxious I am about it,
to see it in print, I believe I would give several years of my
life. I don't care about money, it is only for the pleasure that
I wish it so much.' It is plain that George Moore was
attempting to seduce Ada, and although charmed by him,
she was adamant in resisting. The letters reveal that Ernest
had a jealous nature. Ada writes: 'Your dear letter has a
reproach in it which is not deserved. I know it is hard on
you to give such an alternative. Of course I must see you
again. I am not able to go to the Exhibition today [at Earl's
Court]. I wonder if you could meet me at Madame Tussaud's?
I am less likely to be met there than at the Exhibition where
everyone goes and where my husband might hear of my
being there and if seen with you it would be dangerous . . .
it is a ghastly and fantastic place to meet, but safe. Fancy
discussing our love problems in the Chamber of Horrors!'
In one she writes, surprisingly: 'I wish I were riding with
you on the Downs!'

George Moore had already published several books,
including *Confessions of a Young Man*, but was not yet at the
height of his fame. The following letter of appreciation
from Ada was a forerunner of many others to authors whose
qualities she recognised early, who were destined to become
great celebrities. It relates to a serial by George Moore
appearing in a weekly magazine, and it is evident that Ada
read each instalment with eagerness: 'I am writing again
to tell you how utterly enraptured I am with your last

chapter in the Lady's Pictorial. I really never read anything so good. It is the best of all. That scene, where they are by the fire, recalling their unhappy memories to make themselves still happier and then the letter about Emily, Julia's grief, Hubert's half-insensitivity – that touch of his looking at the newspaper and thinking about the play – and then that last phrase, really it is most exquisite and it does give so perfectly that feeling of worthlessness of life, that feeling that nothing enjoyed is worth the cost of obtaining – that life itself is a doubtful good, full of unattainable ideals, of unsolved problems and ungranted prayers and yet with compensations. Julia must have looked charming in the firelight. Really, Hubert is happier with her than he would have been on that evening with Emily . . . I should like another chapter. How perfectly you have named the story Vain Fortune.'

Her feelings on the subject of the results of a broken marriage are declared in another letter to George Moore and explain why she would never agree to a divorce. She writes: 'I am not afraid of death but I am of scandal, of which I have a special horror. The idea of being talked about is one of which I have a weak terror.'

CHAPTER II

It was in the year 1892 that Ada Leverson met Oscar Wilde for the first time; the occasion was a party given by the first Mrs Oswald Crawfurd, whose husband, a diplomat, was also an important literary figure of the day. The Oswald Crawfurds' parties continued to be a feature of London literary life well into the nineteen hundreds; he became a widower in 1902, then married, as his second wife, an Austrian lady, sister of Lady Brabourne.

At the time of the meeting Ada was ideally conditioned to respond to Wilde's lightheartedness, to his particular form of gaiety illuminated by genius. Wilde found in her no echo but one who had an authentic wit of her own, who, like him, would often express sheer love of fun. Once when Wilde boasted of an apache in Paris who had become so attached to him that he accompanied him everywhere with a knife in one hand, it was characteristic of Ada to reply, 'I'm sure he had a fork in the other!'

Sometimes Oscar would announce himself by telegram thus: 'The author of *The Sphinx* will on Tuesday at two eat pomegranates with the Sphinx of Modern Life' (Ada announced once that Oscar was a master of the wire as a literary medium and it was her intention to edit and bring out a book entitled *The Collected Telegrams of Oscar Wilde*) or by letter: 'Might it be Wednesday or Thursday or Friday? I am just told there are to be feasters here on Tuesday. Do let me know. All my other **days** of the week belong to you. How wilful and wonderful you are!'

Upon discovering that Ada was the author of certain parodies and sketches appearing anonymously in *Punch*, Oscar wrote the following from the Albemarle Club: 'Your sketch is brilliant, as your work always is. It is quite tragic for me to think how completely Dorian Gray has been understood on all sides!

'Why don't you collect your wonderful witty sketches – so slight, so suggestive, so full of *esprit* and intellectual sympathy? You are one of those who in art, are always, by intuition, behind the scenes, so you see how natural art is.'

On July 21, 1894, a parody by Ada of Wilde's poem *The Sphinx* appeared in *Punch*. From then on, he always called her after it, sometimes adding the word 'gilded', perhaps as a tribute to her golden hair, perhaps because of a gilded lily quality he saw in her: 'Dear Sphinx,' he wrote, 'your letter was wonderful and delightful. *The Minx* I long to read. It is a brilliant title. Your feast was rose-like. Quite soon I hope to meet. Oscar.'

It was thought by many that Ada looked a little like Sarah Bernhardt, of whom Wilde was an acknowledged admirer. The likeness is apparent in the portrait of Bernhardt by Bastien Lepage. Ada's features were less regular than those of the actress, but her lips curved more, and the general expression of her face was sweeter and more amiable. In Ada's case this was a true indication of her nature, as even when meeting with opposition to her wishes she would express nothing more than a gentle obstinacy. The charm of her company, it was said, lay in her manner of saying in a low voice unpredictable things ranging from the nonsensical to the wise. 'I don't know that I believe in palmistry, but I *like* it,' was a remark typical of her. Someone starting a conversation with the words: 'Joking apart, – ' was interrupted by

Ada murmuring, 'How dull that sounds! Fancy joking apart, all by oneself.' She once said that a friend who went to a fancy-dress ball as Bacchus would be sure to catch cold as he appeared to be wearing only a grapeskin and a bunch of leopards. On another occasion, a guest excused himself from staying at a party with the plea that it was only by going to bed early that he could keep his youth. 'I didn't know you were keeping a youth,' said Ada. In more serious mood she remarked that envy is the most ageing and wearying factor in life and one should steel oneself in early youth never to feel it. This, it must be said, she succeeded in doing. Jealous in love and friendship she often was, but envious never.

Meeting Wilde had been an event which restored Ada's good spirits and inspired her to write several stories for *Black and White* and *St Stephen's Review*. In one of these she shows that in 1893 the interest in photography was almost as great as in 1963. In another, one is surprised to read of electric shock treatment:

'Where's Leonard?'

'He is in the dark room developing Miss Sinclair.'

'He is fonder than ever of photography. I call him my guide, photographer and friend.'

Leonard is also an amateur doctor; nothing delighted him so much as trying a new medicine or a new system. Someone asks:

'Has Leonard a new . . . ?'

'Oh yes, He's got a freezing machine from Paris which cures rheumatism and he's quite mad on electricity. It's wonderful for neuralgia. You won't mind having a few shocks just to please him, will you? It's really not unpleasant.'

On December 30 of the same year another of her stories appeared in which she wrote:

'Violet is busy arranging her Christmas Cards. She tries to make them appropriate – a task beyond me. I don't understand the theory of it. Why should a card with rough edges be considered suitable to the artistic, robins in snow to the young, and something religious – more or less frosted or even in extreme cases with paper lace – for one's aunts? She tried to persuade us to play Dumb Crambo or to dress up. Nobody entered into her views and she had to be content with pulling a cracker by herself. It didn't even go off properly. In it was a motto with these beautiful words:

> *If I love you as you love me*
> *No knife shall cut our love in two.*
> *The roses blue, the violet red,*
> *Sugar is so, and you are sweet.*

There must have been a misprint as it didn't rhyme. Certainly there seemed something wrong about it.'

Ada saw a wry humour in the condition of those who have expensive tastes without the money to satisfy them, and she would enjoy telling of a young man who, although a bankrupt, continued to run up bills; when his father remonstrated with him the son complained: 'It's bad enough not having any money, but am I not to have anything else *either*?' A similar situation is recounted in another story of hers which appeared in *Black and White*, in which a young man announces: 'I have now nothing on earth but debts, and not even many of those. I have given up hansom cabs. You don't know what that costs me.'

'What, the cabs?'

'No, the sacrifice.'

Ada would speak of the extraordinary aura of kindliness which emanated from Oscar Wilde and which subjugated all with whom he came in contact; of the ability he had to exalt the ordinary doings of life and turn them into exciting adventures. There are instances, too, of his healing quality; those who were unhappy were soon comforted in his presence.

To Ada he appeared a man who made others feel at their best, who cared for his fellow creatures and wished to do good. Linked with these qualities was a fatal exhibitionism. But even those who disliked his long hair, suspected him of being a charlatan, and disapproved of artists, were often won over by his brilliant conversational powers. Wilfred Blunt writes in his diaries: 'He [Wilde] was without exception the most brilliant talker I have ever come across, the most ready, the most witty, the most audacious . . . Nobody could pretend to outshine him, or even to shine at all in his company. Something of his wit is reflected in his plays, but very little. The fine society of London and especially the "Souls" ran after him because they knew he could always amuse them, and the pretty women allowed him great familiarities although there was no question of love-making.' This last remark appears a little sweeping as Oscar, on many occasions, had been the lover of women, and had, according to Ada, a warm and human appeal to those he liked. She would emphasise in later years that, contrary to the impression so often given of him, there was a robustness about his personality. When discussing Oscar she would say that his remarkable gifts and personality could not be gauged by his published works. Had his career not been cut short by disaster he would have given to the world literature infinitely finer than anything he has left us. Those to whom he talked spontaneously recognised genius in him. He would then be sparkling and revealing in his wit in a way that he could not be in the elaborately contrived dialogue of his plays.

It is not surprising that Ada was dazzled by her new friend. Ernest also enjoyed the general glamour of Oscar's society and did not then object to his wife incurring large bills at expensive dressmakers, such as Worth, Paquin and Madame Poutz. The details of one particular purchase remain: a white chiffon tea gown edged with sable, costing forty guineas; a prodigious sum then, but Oscar inspired extravagance. A hairdresser would come to the house from Truefitt's several days a week; on others the French maid would dress her mistress's hair at least twice a day. Hats would be sent from Paris. Letters were exchanged backwards and forwards by hansom cabs or messenger boys. These were summoned by an extraordinary contraption consisting of a bell in a little box in the hall of your house, which communicated with the nearest post office or messenger office; shortly after the bell had been rung, a tiny boy in fancy dress would arrive and be entrusted, possibly, with a priceless communication. Never before, or since, surely, has the respect inspired by a uniform been so strangely demonstrated! Little boys *not* in uniform were treated with great suspicion in those days.

Life then for Ada was a succession of luncheon and dinner parties, first nights and suppers at Willis's Rooms, constantly in the company of the inspiring Oscar and the poet, Lord Alfred Douglas, known to his friend as 'Bosie'. The fashionable puffed sleeves and the pastel-coloured satins and chiffons of the evening dresses of the day were an admirable setting to her fair hair and skin, pale eyes, dark brows and lashes. During this decade Ada formed fascinating friendships. One of these, which for a short time was of importance in the Sphinx's life, was with Prince Henri d'Orléans, explorer and man of action, the grandson of Ferdinand-Philippe, duc d'Orléans, who lost his life tragically in a carriage accident, and of whom Ingres painted so magnificent a portrait. Prince Henri was a complete contrast to Oscar Wilde. One wonders if they ever met; they were to die within a year of each other.

Prince Henri's good looks, courage, intelligence, and ardent imagination made him a figure almost of romance.

The Marquis Boni de Castellane, always a great dandy, writes a little critically of Prince Henri in his memoirs: '. . . I remember him with feelings of real affection. He was gay and handsome, although one of the most untidy individuals imaginable.' To this weakness, if it can so be called, must be added another. Prince Henri loved gambling, an amusement which brings together people so widely different that without it, they would have been unlikely to meet. It was through this interest that Ernest became his friend and that of his cousin. Ada seldom had anything in common with Ernest's gambling friends, but Prince Henri was different. His other interests included writing and in this he found Ada most sympathetic. She was twenty-eight when they met and he twenty-three and already the owner of a gold medal awarded by the Geographical Society. In his book *De Paris au Tonkin au Travers le Thibet Inconnu,* he expresses an intense admiration for the Far East. The book ends with these, perhaps prophetic words: 'Be Asiatic, there lies the future!' Ada noticed in him what she called 'the upward look', seldom seen in the eyes of gamblers. She always interpreted it to mean that the owner cared for an art, an idea, or an ideal. She often spoke of this look; it can be said with truth that Ada never really cared for anyone who was without it. An episode recorded by Baron Lafaurie* reveals how this look, which subjugated Ada, irritated Prince Henri's friends of the theatre and the demimonde. At a dinner-party one night, Louise Marsey, of the Comédie Française, noticed an abstracted expression on Prince Henri's face. This piqued her into saying mockingly to him: 'Eh, Tonkin-Siam! *Laisse un peu ton Indo-Chine et occupe-toi de nous!*' In the same *Souvenirs* there is a glimpse of a life in Paris in which Ernest sometimes took part. One reads of poker-parties on Sundays at the house of Emil Roux in the Rue

* *Mes Souvenirs,* Baron Lafaurie. Les Editions de France, 1937.

Lauriston, where Prince Henri would often be found, when not on some expedition, as well as the duc Decazes, Robert de Flers, the dramatist, usually accompanied by beautiful women. Sometimes Lina Cavalieri, the most exquisite of beauties, then young and unknown, would sing Italian songs to the gamblers when they had tired of their play.

Prince Henri was extremely popular at that time when the French were very Indo-China and Tonkin-conscious. Everyone was humming the words of the song *La Petite Tonkinoise*. The impresario Mr Gilbert Miller still remembers when, as a boy in 1897, he was bathing in the Seine and narrowly escaped being shot by a bullet fired by Prince Henri, who was fighting a duel nearby. His opponent was the Prince de Turin, who had felt personally insulted by certain criticisms of Italian officers in Abyssinia which Prince Henri had made in one of his books. The injuries to both parties were slight.

Ada kept a photograph of Prince Henri near her for the rest of her life and always spoke of him with deep affection.

At a function typical of the time, a *conversazione* at the Royal Water Colour Society, a budding young publisher asked to be presented to Ada. This was Grant Richards. Her mind was so full of the brilliance of her other friends and admirers at that time that she hardly took in his personality at all. Had she known that his recognition of her gifts and his tenacity were going to turn her into a novelist, and that one day she was to see him too in a romantic light, their first meeting would not have been almost completely erased from her mind as it was. Grant Richards does not underestimate her when he writes: 'An introduction to Mrs Ernest Leverson was one of the most important things that could happen to a young man at that time,' and he goes on to describe her as 'the Egeria of the whole Nineties movement, the woman whose wit provoked wit in others, whose intelli-

gence helped so much to leaven the dullness of the period . . .'*
'Caught in the net of her jade eyes', to use Oscar's words in a
letter† some years later, his aim was to entice her to write a
novel. It was nearly twelve years before she would listen
to him.

The ladies of the Leverson family could not understand
Ada's life at that time. They were shocked because at her
luncheon parties there were always more men than women:
'Gentlemen at luncheon, able to visit in the daytime!'
they exclaimed to each other. Drives in the Park, afternoon
calls, long dinner parties, receptions, and an occasional
'drawing-room' with a tea party before or after to show
off their feathers and trains, were the extent of their lives
of pleasure. They failed to see how Ada, with a diamond
merchant as father-in-law, could be indifferent to jewelry. 'It
lasts so long,' she would complain and either sold, lost, or
gave away many beautiful jewels with no regrets, except
for the scenes with Ernest which ensued. In this, one's
sympathies are with him.

Julian, her bachelor brother-in-law, was a man of the
world. He recognised the distinction of being one of Oscar
Wilde's chosen friends but he was wise enough to suspect
that the friendship was a precarious one. Julian was too
conventional to fit in to Ada's côterie of the moment. She
was fond of him but deplored the limitations of his conversation. As a compliment to her connection with literature,
invariably his first question to her would be: 'Have you
read anything pretty lately?' This would be followed by
the statement: 'My plans are these'; and he would go on to
tell of the trains and boats he intended to catch to arrive
eventually at Aix-les-Bains or Homburg. Ernest, like his

* *Memories of a Mis-Spent Youth*, by Grant Richards, William Heinemann,
1932.
† See letter to Robert Ross March 25 1898, *The Letters of Oscar Wilde*,
edited and published by Rupert Hart-Davis, 1962.

Prince Henri d'Orléans

Evelyn Behrens

brother, was devoid of a sense of humour; he was, unlike
Julian, enthusiastic, restless, reckless, and capable of acting on
chivalrous impulses.

It can be said with truth that for a few years the Sphinx
held a successful literary and artistic salon. Without being
rude or unkind, she managed not to accept invitations from
those she found uninteresting, therefore was seldom under
an obligation to invite any but scintillating or beautiful
people. In her drawing-room there would be serious writers,
witty writers, young men who were merely handsome or
amusing, or both. Fans hung on the walls, exquisitely
painted on silk by Charles Conder; Sickert, Beardsley,
Rothenstein, Ricketts, Shannon and Sargent were among the
painters of the day who would visit her. Sometimes the
duc d'Orléans, Prince Henri's cousin, would provide the
glamour that royalty, even in exile, can bring to an occasion.
Few musicians came to the house, but one who did was
Paolo Tosti, the composer and singing teacher, whose
manner had in it a combination of cosiness and mockery which
made him irresistible. He was the original of the character
Sir Tito Landi, in the novel *Love at Second Sight*. This is
how he is described in it: 'With his white moustache, pink
and white complexion, and large bright blue eyes, his
dandified dress, his eyeglass and buttonhole, he had the
fresh, fair look of an Englishman, the dry brilliance of a
Parisian, the naïveté of genius, the manners of a courtier, and,
behind it all, the diabolic humour of the Neapolitan.' Tosti
was the only intimate friend whom Ada shared with any
of her family. One or two of his songs were dedicated to
her youngest sister Violet. Often when arriving at an evening
party in those days, Ada would hear a singer shouting at the
top of his or her voice the words of Tosti's most popular
song: 'Goodbye, Goodbye!' which was not an encouraging
welcome. Another musician friend of the Leversons' was the

singer and composer, Isidore de Lara. His good looks and
manner of singing made him attractive to women and hated
by men. Once the Sphinx and Oscar Wilde went together to
a recital of his songs. The hall was nearly empty so they
dreaded talking to the composer after the concert was over.
Oscar, however, saved the situation by saying: 'Isidore de
Lara: *Your* greatest *failure* will always be *greater* than *my*
greatest success. For there will invariably be present Mrs
Leverson and myself.'*

The Sphinx was seldom malicious and generally loyal to
her friends. Sometimes she carried loyalty too far, sometimes
not quite far enough, as in the case of a political hostess of the
day, of whom someone suggested that her hair was not
natural: 'Of course her hair isn't dyed,' said the Sphinx
indignantly, 'but it is just possible that she may darken the
roots a little'.

The brightest star at the Sphinx's parties was Kitty
Savile-Clark, or Kitty Martineau, as she became after her
marriage. She and her sister, who died young, by reason of
their grace, liveliness, beauty, and a tendency to tuberculosis,
recalled the Linley sisters. It is hardly an exaggeration to
say that every man who saw the tall and slender Kitty fell
in love with her; in the opinion of many at that time she
was the most beautiful girl who had ever walked the earth.
(Max Beerbohm was one of the few men who disagreed with
this assessment – he gave the crown of beauty to Lady
Granby, afterwards the Duchess of Rutland.) To be a
great beauty in those days, it must be remembered, it was
necessary to be authentic in every detail. There was no
mascara or eye-shadow, except for actresses and women of
the demimonde. Hair-dye was crude and unbecoming. The
rare, fortunate possessors of classic features, perfect skins
and bodies were therefore idolised.

* *Noble Essences*, Osbert Sitwell, Macmillan, 1950.

Kitty's resemblance to Emma Hamilton inspired her to dress, sometimes, in the manner beloved of the English eighteenth-century portrait painters. Curiously enough she did not arouse jealousy in other women. Lady Alwyne Compton, her sister Lady Rosslyn, and the Sphinx were her devoted friends, who themselves felt beautified in the radiance she cast. Kitty had many offers of brilliant worldly marriages, all of which she refused, to marry for love the handsome Cyril Martineau. Because of this unspectacular marriage and her death soon after it, Kitty Martineau has been forgotten. She has, however, significance in this story. She was the 'onlie begetter' of the heroines in Ada's six novels, all of whom were, like Kitty, beautiful, fairly intelligent, sweet-natured, devoid of malice and ambition and only concerned with love. The exception to this is Edith Ottley, the chief character of *Love's Shadow*, *Tenterhooks* and *Love at Second Sight*. In the words of Colin MacInnes: 'Edith Ottley, three times a heroine, may best seem, as we know now, to personify – insofar as any character does, or can – its creator, the woman Ada Leverson felt herself to be.' Perhaps the ineffable Kitty has descendants who have inherited her beauty. Her photograph can still be seen in albums, or silver-framed, in some of the great houses of England.

In the circles of the most selective there are often to be found one or two of their intimates whose presence is a mystery, who appear to have been propelled there by an unknown force. For example, Violet Hunt, the novelist, could not have been less to the taste of the Sphinx, who chose her few women friends for their delicacy of mind, or for their beauty either of face or personality. Violet Hunt was coarse and plain, with a skin like leather. At the age of eighteen she must have possessed some beauty or Oscar Wilde would not have called her, as he did in a letter to her mother, 'the sweetest Violet in England.' After the age of thirty she managed the difficult feat of being both spinsterish and intolerant of others, while living openly with the writer Ford Madox Hueffer, who was already married. (He later changed his name to Ford Madox Ford.) Previously, Violet Hunt had had a love affair with Oswald Crawfurd, who, it will be remembered, was also married. Her novels are not uninteresting; they succeed in leaving 'a nasty taste in the mouth', which may account for their success. One wonders why the Sphinx saw her frequently and always went to the garden-parties which she gave on Campden Hill. In some ways she symbolised the New Woman on a bicycle, except that these were depicted in *Punch* as pretty.

Father John Gray, the poet-priest, who is said by some to have inspired Aubrey Beardsley to become a Roman Catholic, was a friend of the Sphinx, André Raffalovich another. The mother of this rich young Russian had been so appalled by his ugliness as a baby that she resolved never to see him again and appointed an English lady to take her place. This was the explanation of the presence of the lady who helped him to entertain his guests in a large house in Mayfair.

Raffalovich was a writer himself and most generous to artists and authors when they were in financial difficulties. In Harry Melvill, the aesthete who has been twice immortalised, once in a diabolic caricature by Max Beerbohm and again in a short story by Osbert Sitwell called 'The Machine Breaks Down,' the Sphinx found one whose conversation really amused her. He would have been more at home in the eighteenth century, his appearance suggesting a white wig, three-cornered hat and a brocade coat, all of which he would put on at the slightest excuse for wearing fancy dress. There was nothing cosy about him as there was about the two Reggies, the Sphinx's most constant companions. Reggie Temple, whose favourite joke was talking Cockney, is the original of the character Vincy Wenham Vincy, who is always being announced at moments of crises, producing a calming effect, in the novel *Tenterhooks*. Vincy's description serves as an exact one of Reggie Temple: 'He had pale silky hair, a minute fair moustache, a single eye-glass and the appearance always of having been very recently taken out of a bandbox. But when people fancied from this look of his that he was an empty-headed fop, they soon found themselves immensely mistaken.' The other, Reggie Turner, is well-known to all students of the life and letters of Wilde. He was an ugly, blinking, twinkling man, a witty conversationalist and a faithful friend with a particular charm of his own.

In the Nineties, Dieppe was a centre for French and English artists and writers. Ada would go there for August and have an enjoyable time with her favourite friends. Fascinating characters, too, such as Comte Robert de Montesquiou and the pianist Léon Delafosse, originals of Proust's Charlus and Charlie Morel, could be seen at the Casino and on the beach. Never before had French food and smells been so much appreciated by sophisticated English people. For many years up to the First World War, the taste of roast chicken and salad at Calais, Boulogne and Dieppe station restaurants held magic for the English traveller.

Among the artists who frequented Dieppe were Jacques Emile Blanche, his friends Baron Adolphe de Meyer, the photographer, and his wife Olga, William Nicholson and James Pryde. An episode which amused the Sphinx occurred some years later when James Pryde painted the portrait of Lady Ottoline Morrell. From the start the artist could not make up his mind what his model should wear; at each sitting she appeared in a different costume, five or six in all, until he settled at last on the most elaborate one. Lady Ottoline was not allowed to look at the portrait until it was finished. When she did see it she was a little disappointed that it was of huge grey stone walls, herself only a little blob of paint at the foot of one.

Max Beerbohm would spend August in Dieppe in the company of the actress, Constance Collier, to whom he became engaged but never married. She was one of those so-called beauties whose short upper lip reached almost to her nostrils. Years later, when she had given up being a beauty, she revealed herself in Somerset Maugham's play *Our Betters* as a superb comedy actress. Max Beerbohm and Ada had been close friends ever since she saw him first at a dancing class – she nearly grown-up and he a little boy in a sailor-suit. She would often tell of how sweet he looked when holding out his white trousers in an attempt to curtsey. They were taught dancing and deportment by the Italian ballerina Taglioni, who was born in 1804, and kept a dancing school after her retirement from the stage until her death in 1884. She may have been the first famous dancer to wear her dark hair parted in the middle and looped over the ears. Max fell in love with Ada while he was at Oxford; in a letter he compared her mouth to 'a little red boat with white sailors in it.'

On one of the rare occasions when the Sphinx went to the Opera, she fainted during the performance. On regaining consciousness, she was surprised to find herself in a small drawing-room, being offered a flask by a flunkey who was saying in an awe-struck voice: 'It's 'is Royal 'Ighness's own brandy!' There, standing at the door, was the Prince of Wales himself, who had seen her collapse and arranged for her to be carried to the ante-room of the royal box. When Ernest appeared he was astonished to see his wife in close conversation with the heir to the Throne. She enjoyed the memory of this episode; suggesting, as it then did to her, a story of Prince Florizel in the *New Arabian Nights*.

Every season, Ada's parents rented a box at Covent

Garden; so did her sister Sybil. Hers was always the same one—close to the stage in the Grand Tier. The splendour of the love duets in Puccini's operas had a special significance for Sybil; often she would listen to them with the composer by her side. It was during one opera season that Mrs Beddington had one of her most discerning 'flashlights'. 'Does David *like* Puccini?' she asked no one in particular: David was Sybil's husband. On the death of the composer many hundreds of letters from him to Sybil came to light, revealing an intimacy the warmth of which no one had suspected, which began in 1904 and continued until his death in 1924.*

It was the era when Mrs Patrick Campbell, Mrs Bernard Beere, affectionately known as 'Bernie' to her friends, and Mrs Cora Brown-Potter originated a new type of beautiful married actress. Unlike their predecessors, such as Mrs Siddons, they were ladies from the upper middle class, whose reputations were only vaguely erotic; they were therefore warmly welcomed in drawing-rooms; Mrs Patrick Campbell, a great friend of the Sphinx, perhaps more warmly than the other two, who, also only vaguely, had a reputation for lesbianism.

Others in the Leversons' world at that time were the famous theatrical married couples, the actor managers who, at one time or another, acted in, or produced Oscar Wilde's plays. Of these the Beerbohm Trees were the most interesting. Herbert Beerbohm Tree revealed in his manner, appearance, and acting, a touch of genius. Maud, his wife, was original and witty. She shares with Ada Leverson, Mrs Patrick Campbell and Lady Oxford the honour of having had her sayings repeated and quoted again and again. The disadvantage of a reputation for wit is that the witticisms get mixed up and are attributed to the wrong people. Mrs Patrick Campbell is now believed to have observed that

* *Puccini. A Critical Biography*, Mosco Carner, Duckworth, 1958.

Lady Tree was one of those on whom real ermine looked like rabbit. The truth is that it was said by the Sphinx. Lady Tree was one of the 'Souls', although not in their inner circle. A clever and endearing trait in her character was the lighthearted manner with which she treated her husband's infidelity. It was said that when someone suggested that she buy a dog and train it to bark at every woman to whom Beerbohm Tree paid attention, Lady Tree replied that this ruse had been tried but the poor dog had died of sleeplessness.

The least exotic of the fashionable theatrical married couples were Mr and Mrs Cyril Maude; he was born a country gentleman and retained the tastes of one. They were a devoted couple, very popular with their fellow actors and actresses.

George Alexander had no natural gifts other than his good looks. He was taught, most successfully, every gesture, every expression and tone of voice to use on the stage by Sir Henry Irving. His wife was wildly extravagant in her dress, and would wear paradise plumes on jauntily-tilted hats, feather boas and long strings of pearls, at all times. This bad taste hid a kind heart.

Of all the galaxy of talent, and it was a period rich in glamorous theatrical figures, the Sphinx's favourite actor was Charles Hawtrey. He was neither good-looking nor romantic. Yet the naturalistic manner of his acting illuminated everything he did on the stage. It was her dream to write a play for him. Seeing one in Paris which she thought would be easy to adapt for the English stage, Ada persuaded Ernest to buy the dramatic rights. It satirised a shallow, cynical, frivolous group of people who were supposed to behave as they did because they were living at the *fin de siècle*. The Sphinx called her version *The Triflers* and worked on it in a desultory fashion for more than twenty years. She ignored the dialogue of the French original and wrote her own. The play was altered very slightly, again and again. In the first version there was a duchess and a conservatory, as in the plays of Wilde. One scene satirises the pose of morbidity adopted by some at that time. In a conversation between a young married woman and her lover, she pretends to believe that double suicide is the only solution to all true love problems, and is always urging him towards this end; he is bored and complains that he has not got the time, also that he would have to resign from his club, the Marlborough, were he to do what she asks.

HARRY: I don't feel like it, I'm depressed.

SILVIA: But you still feel the same about me?

HARRY: More so, if anything.

SILVIA: Then what about Tuesday week?

HARRY: My dear, I was just going to write to you! I made a muddle of my engagements. I can't, not on Tuesday, it's the dance, you know, at Worcester House.

SILVIA: Oh yes, I forgot. But what about the next day?

HARRY: My dear, what's that day? Wednesday – oh – Wednesday I can't. I'm dining out.

SILVIA: Dining out? Fancy letting a trivial engagement like that . . .

HARRY: I was always taught that a dinner engagement is a sacred engagement.

SILVIA: Well – where are you dining, if I may ask?

HARRY: You may ask and what is more, I'll tell you. I'm dining with your husband at the Club.

SILVIA: My husband! Oh, so you let *him* come between us.

HARRY: But isn't he the only one who has the right to?

SILVIA: But if we put it off too long it will fall perfectly flat. What will all those heartless brutes at Deauville care for our troubles? Why, even my husband will be yachting . . .

The dialogue continues in this lively way during the

whole of the play; the plot, although slight, is ingenious. The last version was made in the late Twenties for the ageing Mrs Patrick Campbell. By that time, the Duchess and the conservatory had been dropped, and taxis, telephones, and mentions of the Sitwells and Noel Coward had been added. The play was never quite finished and Ada failed to achieve her ambition to hear her words spoken on the stage by Charles Hawtrey, or indeed by any one else.

CHAPTER III

The Green Carnation, published in 1894, was a novel in which the two principal characters are recognisable portraits of Oscar and Bosie. Many suspected the Sphinx of being the author; it was not long, however, before it was discovered that it had been written by Robert Hichens. In a letter from Worthing, Oscar wrote: '. . . of course you have been deeply wronged. But there are many bits in *The Green Carnation* not unworthy of your brilliant pen, and treachery is inseparable from faith; I often betray myself with a kiss. Robert Hichens I did not think capable of anything so clever! . . . It is such a bore about journalists, they are so very clever.

'How sweet of you to have *Intentions* bound for your birthday! I simply love that book.

'I shall be in town soon and must come and charm the Sphinx with honey-cakes. The trouble is I left my flute in a railway carriage and the Fauns take so long to cut new reeds.'

A wonderful opportunity to enhance her reputation presented itself when the editors of *The Yellow Book* invited the Sphinx to be one of its contributors. Although she was not a literary careerist, and wrote for the sheer pleasure of seeing herself in print, the anonymity forced upon the contributors to *Punch* was a little exasperating; naturally the honour of being in the company of some of the greatest writers of the age in *The Yellow Book* was most gratifying.

In the same number in which her first story appeared, there was reproduced an extremely unflattering portrait of her by Walter Sickert. Her two stories, *Suggestion* and *The Quest of Sorrow*, are satires on the young aesthete of the period; a type of no great intelligence, of intense vanity and extreme selfishness; they were young men who, no doubt, had adopted the pose through the influence of Wilde's plays. This genre has never been better parodied than by George S. Street in his *The Autobiography of a Boy*. Ada's stories are a continuation of Street's theme. Insolent and indolent as were some of these men in fiction and in real life, they were by no means all effeminate.

George Street was an intimate friend of the Sphinx. He tried to keep secret what the initial S. stood for; but his secret was uncovered: it stood for Slythe. He was a fat man with a squeaky voice, always in love with some girl or other, whose best known work, *The Ghosts of Piccadilly*, reveals how great a literary craftsman he was. After being dramatic critic on *The Pall Mall Gazette* he became censor of plays. He outlived many of his contemporaries. Although he was an ardent admirer of women, he remained a bachelor.

It has been said that Aubrey Beardsley felt Oscar Wilde patronised him. This may have been the case. Might the cause have been that Oscar saw in Aubrey a rival? Their two names are those most widely known as representatives of the decadents of the Nineties, a decade which is in fact named by many 'the Beardsley Period'. They certainly felt an instinctive antagonism to each other. Oscar wrote later to Ada: 'Have you seen *The Yellow Book?* It is horrid and not yellow at all.' He wrote in a letter to Lord Alfred Douglas that is was dull and loathsome and that he was glad of it. Aubrey, for his part, said in a note to Robert Ross, of Oscar and Bosie: 'They really are rather dreadful people.' (It was ironic that Beardsley, after having designed different covers for its first four volumes, should have been expelled from *The Yellow Book* because his name was associated with the then disgraced Oscar.) When Wilde was arrested, it was recorded in the press that he had *The Yellow Book* under his arm. 'This killed *The Yellow Book*,' wrote John Lane, its publisher, 'and it nearly killed me'.

The pleasure that the Sphinx should have experienced in the publication of her two stories was much diminished by the fact that the first one appeared in April 1895, the month in which Oscar's troubles started. Meanwhile the following interview by her had appeared in *The Sketch* of January 2. It is signed and is entitled *A Few Words with Mr Max Beerbohm*.

'Mr Max Beerbohm left Oxford only last term to plunge into the delights of literature in London. In that short space of time, by his curious contributions to *The Yellow Book*, he has gained a more than merely esoteric fame. Indeed, he may be said to occupy in literature somewhat the same position as does Mr Aubrey Beardsley in art. The success of each has been a success of astonishment. Both are essentially modern, and "implected", to borrow some of Mr Beerbohm's own favourite phrases, with a love of the "mysteries of style", a passion for "paradox and *marivaudage*" – in fact, for "all unusual things". The style of each, moreover, is wonderfully sure and complete for artists so very young.

'I went with a letter of introduction to Mr Beerbohm's house some time ago. It is one of that row of houses known as Hyde Park Place. Its windows command a charming view of the Park – a place which, as Mr Beerbohm remarked to me, is "quite as nice as the country, and not half so provincial". The room in which Mr Beerbohm received me and spends most of his time is the same room in which

Kinglake wrote his famous history of the Crimean War.
I could not help wondering what Kinglake would have
thought of his youthful successor's History of George the
Fourth. Youthful certainly he is – not, indeed, quite as
youthful as he is seen in the portrait which he gave me for
reproduction in *The Sketch*, and which, he explained, is the
only one that has been taken in recent years. [The photograph was of Max as a little boy wearing a sailor suit.] He
has altered very little since then, though he no longer
wears a fringe and has exchanged the frivolities of the white
and blue sailor suit for the sterner realities of the frock-
coat and high collar. His inscrutable, somewhat cynical,
expression heightens his appearance of youthfulness, and his
manners are studiously urbane.

' "I am afraid," he said, in his gentle, musical voice, in
answer to my request, "that there is very little to tell about
my life so far. I have done the ordinary things. I went to
Charterhouse when I was twelve, but I don't know that I
enjoyed myself much there. I agree with that cosy writer, Mr
James Payn, who has so often pointed out that boys are
not a nice race. They are bullies or cowards, according to
their size. Not that there was 'bullying' in the accepted
sense – that has all been suppressed, along with highway
robbery and town-and-gown rows. Boys, nowadays, indulge
in a kind of social terrorism among themselves that is far
more objectionable than the roasting and tossing of the good
old days. The snobbishness of boys is amazing. The gossip
and the scandal that go on at a public school would alarm a
dowager. But Oxford – Oxford is the perfect city. I shall
never have such a happy time as I had there."

' "What are your plans now? Are you going in for literature wholly?" '

' "No; I intend to draw as well – always caricatures. You
may have seen my series in *Pick-Me-Up* and the *Pall Mall*

Budget. One or two of those drawings have been thought rather cruel, I believe. I can't understand how anyone can resent a mere exaggeration of feature. The caricaturist simply passes his subject through a certain grotesque convention. That the result is not a classically beautiful figure proves nothing about the personal appearance of the subject. There is no such thing as a good or a bad subject for caricature. To the true caricaturist Adonis or Punchinello is equally good game. I never pretend that my caricatures are meant for portraits. And I do not think that the men themselves whom I have drawn have ever been offended."

' "Perhaps their wives have been? Now tell me, Mr Beerbohm, about your writing. Tell me about the article on 'Cosmetics' – the best-abused thing in the first number of *The Yellow Book* – or about your white-washing of George IV."

' "My article on 'Cosmetics' was a very good joke, but – I thought when I wrote it – rather obvious. I was surprised the critics did not see it at once. It is not often a new writer has to complain of being taken too seriously. 'George IV' was received in a far more reasonable manner. My point of view was more nearly understood. I meant all I said about George, but I did not choose to express myself quite seriously. To treat history as a means of showing one's own cleverness may be rather rough on history, but it has been done by the best historians, from Herodotus to Froude and myself. Some of my 'George' was false, and much was flippant; but why should a writer sit down to be systematically serious, or else conscientiously comic? Style should be oscillant.'

' "Oscillant? Is that one of your queer words, of which we have heard so much? Do you intend to abandon them, as an affectation?"

' "Certainly not. They are not affected. At times there is no word in the English dictionary by which I can express my shade of meaning. I try to think of a French, or Latin, or

Greek one. If I can't, then I invent a word – such as 'pop-limbo' or 'bauble-tit' – often a compound of some well-known English word with an affix or prefix to point its significance. Sometimes I invent a word merely because the cadence of a sentence demands it."

' "And are you writing much now?"

' "I am doing some work for the new *Saturday Review*, and I am in treaty with a publisher to produce a little book of studies and essays. At this moment I am writing a treatise upon 'The Brothers of Great Men,' including a series of psychological sketches of Mr Willie Wilde, Mr Austen Chamberlain, and others."

' "You are a brother of Mr Beerbohm Tree, I believe?"

' "Yes; he is coming into the series!" '

The beginning of this year 1895 finds the Sphinx in the highest of spirits, her brain fertile in ideas for parodies. Did she not hear some of Oscar's friends asking each other if he were not getting too arrogant and reckless? Testing too much, perhaps, his power to outwit and to charm? She knew nothing of his anxieties, which, characteristically, he was treating with an excess of bravado; to her and doubtless to many others, he was as charming as ever. *The Ideal Husband* was produced on January 3 at the Haymarket Theatre. In reply to the Sphinx's suggestion that she should write a skit upon it for *Punch*, Wilde, who was suffering from a cold, replied in the following telegram:

'8th January, 1895. I am so pleased my dear Sphinx, no other voice but yours is musical enough to echo my music. Your article will be worthy of you and me. Have you a box tomorrow night? If so I will come. I am still forbidden to go out.'

The following parody of *An Ideal Husband* appeared in *Punch* on January 12, 1895, entitled 'Overheard Fragment of a Dialogue'.

LORD ILLINGWORTH: My dear Goring, I assure you that a well-tied tie is the first serious step in life.

LORD GORING: My dear Illingworth, five well-made button-holes a day are far more essential. They please women, and women rule society.

LORD ILLINGWORTH: I understood you considered women of no importance?

LORD GORING: My dear George, a man's life revolves on curves of intellect. It is on the hard lines of the emotions that a woman's life progresses. Both revolve in cycles of master-pieces. They should revolve on bicycles; built, if possible, for two. But I am keeping you?

LORD ILLINGWORTH: I wish you were. Nowadays it is only the poor who are kept at the expense of the rich.

LORD GORING: Yes. It is perfectly comic, the number of young men going about the world nowadays who adopt perfect profiles as a useful profession.

LORD ILLINGWORTH: Surely that must be the next world? How about the Chiltern Thousands?

LORD GORING: Don't, George. Have you seen Windermere lately? Dear Windermere! I should like to be exactly unlike Windermere.

LORD ILLINGWORTH: Poor Windermere! He spends his mornings in doing what is possible, and his evenings in saying what is probable. By the way, do you really understand all I say?

LORD GORING: Yes, when I don't listen attentively.

LORD ILLINGWORTH: Reach me the matches, like a good boy – thanks. Now define these cigarettes – as tobacco.

LORD GORING: My dear George, they are atrocious. And they leave me unsatisfied.

LORD ILLINGWORTH: You are a promising disciple of mine. The only use of a disciple is that at the moment of one's triumph he stands behind one's chair and shouts that after all one is immortal.

LORD GORING: You are quite right. It is as well, too, to remember from time to time that nothing that is worth knowing can be learnt.

LORD ILLINGWORTH: Certainly, and ugliness is the root of all industry.

LORD GORING: George, your conversation is delightful, but your views are terribly unsound. You are always saying insincere things.

LORD ILLINGWORTH: If one tells the truth, one is sure sooner or later to be found out.

LORD GORING: Perhaps. The sky is like a hard hollow sapphire. It is too late to sleep. I shall go down to Covent Garden and look at the roses. Good-night, George! I have had such a pleasant evening!

Three weeks later Ada's parody of *The Importance of Being Earnest* appeared in *Punch*.

THE ADVISABILITY
OF NOT BEING BROUGHT UP IN A HANDBAG
A Trivial Tragedy for Wonderful People
(Fragment found between the St James's and Haymarket Theatres).

TIME – the other day. The Scene is in a garden, and begins and ends with relations.

ALGY (*eating cucumber sandwiches*): Do you know, Aunt Augusta, I am afraid I shall not be able to come to your dinner tonight, after all. My friend Bunbury has had a relapse, and my place is by his side.

AUNT AUGUSTA (*drinking tea*): Really, Algy! It will put my table out dreadfully. And who will arrange my music?

DORIAN: I will arrange your music, Aunt Augusta. I know all about music. I have an extraordinary collection of musical instruments. I give curious concerts every Wednesday in a long latticed room, where wild gipsies tear mad

music from little zithers, and I have brown Algerians who
beat monotonously upon copper drums. Besides, I have set
myself to music. And it has not marred me. I am still the
same. More so if anything.

CICELY: Shall you *like* dining at Willis's with Mr Dorian
tonight, Cousin Algy?

AUNT AUGUSTA: Sweet child! I see distinct social probabilities
in her profile. Mr Dorian has a beautiful nature. And it is
such a blessing to think that he was not brought up in a
handbag like so many young men of the present day.

ALGY: It is such a blessing, Aunt Augusta, that a woman
always grows exactly like her aunt. It is such a curse that a
man never grows exactly like his uncle. It is the greatest
tragedy of modern life.

DORIAN: To be really modern one should have no soul. To be
really mediaeval one should have no cigarettes. To be really
Greek—

(*The Duke of Berwick rises in a marked manner, and leaves
the garden*).

CICELY: (*writes in her diary, and then reads aloud dreamily*):
The Duke of Berwick rose in a marked manner, and left the
garden. The weather continues charming . . .'

While Ada was scintillating and Oscar's affairs were
smouldering, Ernest was occupied in attending race-meetings,
gambling at his clubs, or dashing over to Paris. Sometimes
he wore a blue suit with a small white stripe, which the
Sphinx called his 'Dreyfus suit'; he always seemed to be
wearing it, she observed, when he discussed the case. This
remark typified her detached but affectionate way of laughing
at him. They were an ill-matched couple with few tastes in
common; furthermore, each needed what they had not got,
a partner who knew the true value of money. They existed
in different elements, except on rare occasions. In spite of
unpredictable manifestations, or because of these, Ada

was unaware of the money anxieties which lie behind the scenes in every gambler's life. Soon husband and wife were to be brought together by shared pity and indignation, in circumstances when his lack of a sense of humour would cease for a time to matter.

Alas! Oscar's 'days of gilded infamy,' as he called them when in remorseful mood, were about to come to an end. All who have studied his life know how Ada fetched him from his mother's house and brought him to stay with her between his trials. To one of her compassionate nature it was a simple action and she was fortunate in not being hampered in the execution of her wishes by a cautious husband. There was no difficulty in gaining Ernest's consent. He had frequently demonstrated sympathy with the victimised in the zeal with which he defended Dreyfus whenever the case was discussed. On the day before he arrived at her house, Oscar wrote to the Sphinx:

*[?Early May, 1895]   [? 146 *Oakley Street*]
My dear Sweet Kind Friend, I have no words to thank you for all you do for me, but for you and Ernest Bosie and I have deepest love.

I hope to be in better spirits tonight. Your sweetness last night was wonderful. Your flowers are like him – your sending them like yourself. Dear, dear Friend, tonight I see you at 7.45. Ah! you are good and gentle and wonderful. Always devotedly yours,   Oscar

The fortnight spent by Oscar Wilde in the Leversons' house in Courtfield Gardens, the events which led up to it, and those that succeeded it are told in the Sphinx's own words at the end of this sketch.

* *The Letters of Oscar Wilde*, p. 396, edited and published by Rupert Hart-Davis, 1962.

CHAPTER IV

What followed was hard to bear. Wilde's imprisonment cast a gloom over the lives of those who cared for him; the friendship which had been a source of pride became one to be spoken of in hushed voices. His name was seldom pronounced, initials alone would be used. The scandal was so great that a large portrait of Wilde by Harper Pennington which hung on the walls of the Leversons' house was covered at the time of the trial. (It was the property of the disgraced poet, came up for sale, was bought by Ernest for Wilde and is now in California).

It was not long before the following letter, hitherto unpublished, was received from Alfred Douglas:

Villa Tarnasse
Sorrento

Sept 13th, 1895
Dearest Sphinx,

I have just got your telegram, for which many thanks. I have been made very miserable by receiving the enclosed letter from the Governor of Wandsworth Prison to whom I wrote asking if I might write to Oscar. I can't make it out at all, as it appears from this letter that Oscar *had* the power to correspond with me but that he deliberately preferred not to. Can you throw any light on the question? My anxiety has been added to by the fact that Robert Sherard*

* Robert Harborough Sherard, 1861-1943, author and journalist.

has not written to me, and although I have had letters from you and Bobbie [Robert Ross] and More Adey* since Sherard's interview, you have none of you said a single word about what Oscar said at the interview. It seems to me most heartless and extraordinary of Sherard not to write to me, as I presume that surely Oscar must have sent me some message. I am so upset and perplexed by it all. It seems impossible ever to find out what is really happening. I am so afraid that some secret influence has been brought to bear on Oscar, or that he has been told some lies about me. It seems to me *quite inconceivable* that he should prefer to correspond with his *'family'* than with me without some very strong reason of which I know nothing. Altogether I am in utter misery and despair. Gatty is going away and I shall be left alone again as neither More nor Bobbie will come out to me. I really wish Oscar and I were both dead. I have taken a little villa at Capri, and am going there to-morrow. My address there is

Villa Caso

Strada

Pastana

Capri.

It is a lovely little place but I shall be quite alone there, as Gatty remains here till he goes. Goodbye for the present, dear Sphinx, please write to me often and try and find out the mystery about Oscar.

Ever yours most affectionately,

Bosie.

There is an explanation for Wilde's refusing to correspond with Douglas, and why no-one told Douglas anything about the interview is obvious. After his removal to Wandsworth on July 4, 1895, Wilde was allowed to write only one letter

* William More Adey, 1858-1942, a close friend of Robert Ross.

every three months, and the first was certainly to his wife and his lawyers. Douglas's suspicions that Wilde had been told some lies about him were well-founded. Robert Sherard had warned Wilde, when visiting him in August, that Douglas was about to publish all Wilde's letters to him in an article for the *Mercure de France*. Wilde told Sherard to prevent its appearance, which he did. In fact, Douglas had written the article in passionate defence of his friend, with the best of intentions and in the hope of rehabilitating him. But as the project was presented by Sherard, it appeared shocking to Wilde that his most intimate feelings were to be revealed to the world.

Soon the Sphinx was to suffer from Oscar's fluctuating emotions, not regarding herself, for whom he repeatedly expressed affection, but towards her husband. When in prison Oscar turned against Ernest, ceasing to feel any gratitude to the friend who had produced money for the trial at a few hours' notice, to whom he had written at the time: '. . . Bosie and I cannot sufficiently thank you for your great kindness to us: we shall never forget it, but shall always cherish in affection and gratitude the friend who at a moment's notice came forward to help us, so gracefully, so kindly, so readily. In a few days we hope to be free of our monetary obligations . . .

This change began when Oscar's obsession with money first showed itself. Alfred Douglas writes with gratitude about Ernest in his autobiography. He observes that Wilde, towards the end of his sentence and after his release, lost nearly all sense of honesty and honour. Although Alfred Douglas is not always reliable in his statements, he knew Wilde well enough to make the right appraisal of his behaviour on the subject of money at that time. Ernest visited Oscar in prison, met him on his release, wrote a full statement of his financial dealings and refused to be offended by one who had so greatly suffered. The situation was a painful one for the Sphinx, who knew that tact was not Ernest's strong point, but that Oscar's accusations were unjust. Luckily there was the task of moving house to occupy her thoughts. South Kensington had been a popular neighbourhood with young couples in the Eighties, but at the beginning of the next decade, the Sphinx felt it to be too far out. In those days of horse-drawn carriages it took some time to reach the best shops and the theatres from Courtfield Gardens, whereas Deanery Street, off Park Lane and opposite Stanhope Gate, lay in the heart of London. The prospect and the achievement of living there produced in the Sphinx a feeling of elation. Even the shops in South Audley Street – especially Cecil Roy, theatre ticket and messenger office – seemed to have a magic, an inconsequent gaiety about them which suited her particular temperament. She looked forward to receiving Oscar in her new house after his release.

Francis Burnard, *Punch's* editor, had noticed with regret the cessation of sketches and parodies from the Sphinx's pen. He therefore wrote a note urging her to contribute regularly again; he added this little jingle, which scans as badly as a motto out of a cracker: 'Changing the scenery, gone to the Deanery, Leafery Greenery, but word of good omen, *où je dinerai*'. It had the desired effect and the parodies and stories were resumed.

Max Beerbohm had offered advice about the decoration of the new house: '19, Hyde Park Place, W. My dearest Mrs Leverson, I shall be quite charmed to come tomorrow and look forward to seeing Bob——. (?)

'1. I should have a slim Queen Anne sort of sofa and chairs in the back room – (is it big enough for any sofa?) or perhaps rather I should have the same satinwood chairs as in the big room – by the way I think the small chairs should be covered with dark green silk – or are you having everything chintz ?

'II. Green curtains for the back room—or how would white silk be, or *pale blue* silk ? Perhaps a pale blue curtain between the rooms but one must see the colours – mind the wall green is dingy green – as dark as that book – Yours till tomorrow, Max.'*

His advice was followed in a small back room on the ground floor, the walls of which were covered in green linen. Those of the double drawing-room were decorated in blue and white damask. The Conder fans were again hung, otherwise there were few pictures in the room. A set of Japanese prints were over the staircase. The furniture was Louis xv, with the addition of a white baby grand piano on which the Sphinx would play, slightly inaccurately and by ear, Chopin, Strauss, popular waltzes of the day, such as *Valse Bleu* and *Amoureuse*, tunes from *The Belle of New York* and from contemporary musical comedies. The frequent sound of music spread light-heartedness among those surrounding her. Stanhope Gate and Hyde Park could be seen from the windows. The clip-clop of hansom cabs and carriages added to the liveliness. The Sphinx would laugh when commiserated with on the continual sound of traffic. It was true that Deanery Street was a short cut to Park Lane and did attract more traffic than most streets. One got accustomed to it, she would say, as one does to the sound of the sea. If there were illness in any of the houses, straw would be laid down in the streets to deaden the sound of horses' hooves. Otherwise the noise was busy, but not unpleasant.

The whole house was decorated in blue and white, excepting the front door, which was painted the colour of an emerald. All the bedrooms of the little Regency house had powder closets leading out of them; the windows of the upper

* Quoted in *A Study in Yellow*, by Katherine Lyon Mix, Constable, 1960.

floors looked directly over the gardens of Dorchester
House and that of Mrs Bishoffsheim. One might be awakened
on a spring or summer night, and lulled to sleep again,
by the music of a blue Hungarian Band playing for the delight
of guests at a ball; in the day-time the sounds made by a
barrel organ would suggest rakish jollity or inspire fears of
unknown squalor. Mayfair symbolised gaiety to the Sphinx
and the very air invigorated her. When she gave dinner
parties, the table would be decorated by a florist with
smilax and carnations or small roses. On the hall table, top
hats, some of them smelling sweetly of hair-oil, would
frequently be found at luncheon time, and the sound of loud
laughter would come from the dining-room.

Scent was much used by dandies on their hair and by
women of bad reputation. Ladies seldom wore anything
stronger than lavender water or that mysterious and rather
unpleasant scent known as orris root. Real and imitation
bunches of Parma violets were much worn at that time,
often pinned to a fur. The Sphinx's favourite scent was that
of gardenias, a spray of which she would wear whenever
possible.

The drawing-room mantelpiece would be cluttered with
invitation and race-cards; Ernest, to his ultimate ruin, was an
enthusiastic follower of the turf. A scrap of dialogue from
Ada's first novel, *The Twelfth Hour*, gives the atmosphere:

'Don't you know by this time that whenever Chetwode
is particularly wanted, he is sure to be either at Kempton or
Christie's?'

'Spending at Christie's what he's lost at Kempton I
suppose.'

The racing losses were succeeded by losses in the City.
Ernest's outbursts of temper became more frequent. Often,
when dressed to go out to dinner together, the Sphinx
would be sent back to her room in tears to scrub her face

free from suspected rouge. A diamond necklace was stolen, causing the house to be full of detectives and suspicion to fall upon the French maid and the window-cleaner. Both were exonerated, but the Sphinx was scolded. Ernest was one of those husbands who become angry with their wives when things go wrong. The loss of anything valuable put him into a bad temper because his wife's indifference made her, in his eyes, to blame. She was encouraged to have everything she bought put down to his account. This resulted in large bills, and scenes when they were presented; when asked if there were any other bills, she would lie to prevent more scenes; this led to a real explosion. Luckily, the Deanery Street house had a hypnotic charm for her, which made up for these disturbances.

The day after Oscar's release from prison he wrote this moving letter:

20 May, 1897   Hotel Sandwich, Dieppe.
Dear Sphinx,

I was so charmed with seeing you yesterday morning that I must write a line to tell you how sweet and good it was of you to be of [*sic*] the very first to greet me. When I think that Sphinxes are minions of the moon and that you got up early before dawn, I am filled with wonder and joy.

I often thought of you in the long black days and nights of my prison-life, and to find you just as wonderful and dear as ever was no surprise. The beautiful are always beautiful.

This is my first day of real liberty, so I try to send you a line, and with kind regards to dear Ernest, whom I was pleased to see again.

                    Ever affectionately yours,
                                        Oscar Wilde.

I am staying here as Sebastian Melmoth – not Esquire but Monsieur Sebastian Melmoth – I have thought it better that Robbie should stay here under the name of Reginald Turner, and Reggie under the name of R. B. Ross. It is better that they should not have their own names.

Later, Wilde wrote to Robert Ross saying that he had received a sweet letter from the Sphinx telling him Ernest's name had appeared in the newspapers as a co-respondent in a divorce case. Ernest, it seems, had subscribed to a press cutting agency and was disappointed with his notices! 'Considering the growing appreciation of Ibsen, I must say that I am surprised the notices were not better. But nowadays everybody is jealous of everyone else, except of course husband and wife . . . I think I shall keep this last remark of mine for my play,' Oscar observed. The Sphinx forgave her husband and appeared with him in public, as conspicuously as possible, the day after the case was reported.

In 1898 there arose an excuse for the Sphinx to go to see Oscar in Paris. At the time of his trial he had entrusted her with the manuscript of his play *La Sainte Courtisane*. It was only natural to insist on returning it to its author with her own hands. It is a pity that more is not known of the last meeting between Oscar and the Sphinx other than her distress on seeing how much he had deteriorated in appearance and health, and the episode of his leaving the manuscript in a cab directly after it had been restored to him. 'A cab,' he said, 'is a very proper place for it.'

In her copy of *The Importance of Being Earnest*, in 1899, he wrote the following: 'To the wonderful Sphinx to whose presence on the first night, the success of this comedy was entirely due. From her friend her admirer, who wrote it, Oscar Wilde'.

The news of his death in Paris came as a great shock to all who knew him.

Oscar Wilde had had a strong influence upon the Sphinx. He had been the catalyst necessary to the full development of her personality. With him she had known an exciting fulfilment in the realm of the mind. Who was there to sparkle back at him better than herself? His appreciation was a gift which she treasured for a life-time. It had polished the precious stone of her own talent. Perhaps, had she never known Wilde's admiration, she would not have had the confidence necessary for the writing of her novels. Less good was his influence in other ways. The Sphinx had been brought up in ignorance of the value of money. She thought that as a matter of course it would always be there because her father was a rich man. It was her misfortune that she knew nothing of the practical side of life. Oscar had led her even further away from it. To be told, 'You are one of those, alas too few, who are always followed by the flutes of the pagan world,' would encourage almost anyone to be uninterested in the prosaic things of life. She had never used her small hands, with their tapering fingers and almond-shaped nails, for any elementarily useful purposes such as putting away her clothes, tying up a parcel, or boiling a kettle; there had been no need. Later, when the knowledge of such simple skills would have been of invaluable use to her, it was too late.

The Sphinx felt a chill of loneliness as one after another of the friends who had shed brightness upon her life died; Aubrey Beardsley at Mentone in 1898, at the pathetically early age of twenty-four; Prince Henri, in 1901, from the effects of dysentery at Saigon, only ten years older (his mother lived on until 1925 in the beautiful château of St Firmin, at Chantilly, where in the woods there stands a monument to his memory). In her growing need for sym-

pathetic companionship, the Sphinx would visit Robert
Ross most days at the Carfax Gallery, in Ryder Street,
knowing for sure that he would be found there. If he thought
her visits excessive, he did not tell her so. It was characteristic
of her, this need to know what was going on, to exchange
ideas with an intelligent human being. It was the need that
men have which causes them to 'look in' daily at their
clubs. Later, the Sphinx would go to Hatchard's book shop
in Piccadilly where stimulating conversations with Arthur
Humphries would be the attraction.

Robert Ross had started the Carfax Gallery for the
exhibition of the works of new artists. The list of those
whose pictures were shown there for the first time contains
many great names.

A year after the death of Oscar, the Sphinx's spirits rose
a little when her friend Max Beerbohm achieved success.
His caricatures dazzled and startled the world from the walls
of the Carfax Gallery at the same time as his play, *The
Happy Hypocrite*, in which Mrs Patrick Campbell and George
Arliss acted, enchanted audiences.

Robert Ross had set himself the task of putting Wilde's
posthumous affairs in order for the benefit of his sons; he
succeeded in doing this by reviving the interest of the public in
the books and plays which had been banned in 1895; also
by bringing out the first incomplete edition of *De Profundis*;
in doing so Ross made an implacable enemy of Alfred
Douglas. All this is common knowledge; but only those who
knew the Sphinx well could realise how deeply she felt the
persecution of one of her friends by another. She loved and
truly admired Robbie's character and hated to see him
suffer; Alfred Douglas was adamant in his hatred and spread
libellous stories about Ross. It is strange that he did not
turn against the Sphinx, as he knew whose side she was on
in the quarrel.

Three more habitués of the Sphinx's drawing-room should be mentioned, although they were of little importance in her life. Douglas Ainslie, for one, was a poet and friend of Proust, with an exaggerated affected manner of talking. Claud Nugent and Scrobby Ponsonby were two others. These men were both very tall and had loud voices and hearty laughs of a kind which was very frightening to a child. What could have inspired their roars of merriment? The Sphinx's form of wit called more, one would have thought, for smiles.

Several years later the Sphinx received a shattering blow. Ernest discovered that he had lost nearly all his money in some business enterprise in the City. His father agreed to settle his debts and to give him a fresh start in the timber business in Canada, where it was hoped he would be far enough away from race-meeting, clubs, Deauville and Monte Carlo not to be tempted to gamble. There was no question of Ada and her little daughter accompanying him. (Their son had died, to their sorrow.) Ernest's illegitimate daughter, however, to Ada's great relief, was only too ready to take care of her father; they embarked together to live contentedly in Canada for the rest of his life. The saddest part of this change was that the Sphinx had to leave the lovely little house which she had found so harmonious with her temperament. Soon another one, built about 1840, was found near enough to Hyde Park Square to enable Miss Hudson, her father's secretary-housekeeper, to manage the practical side of her life. This kindly interference was something the Sphinx loathed. But what was she to do? With only her dowry to live upon and not the slightest idea how to manage her household economically, she was helpless, and also suffered much in restraining her generous impulses.

Once settled in Radnor Place, Hyde Park, her white baby grand piano looking a little too large for its new environment,

the Sphinx tried to look on the bright side of her new life.
Conversation was her great amusement and there were still
old friends and new ones anxious to supply it. Being the
least self-seeking person imaginable, whose actions were
governed by her heart or by her interest in individuals, she
was incapable of cultivating any acquaintances for an ulterior
motive. The result was that although the number of her
friends was comparatively few, in her company they felt
not only entertained but reassured and safe. She was lazy
by nature, therefore it is much to her credit that she had
disciplined herself to work hard at her writing while living
in Deanery Street and experiencing the agitations of life
with Ernest. She wrote a weekly column for women in
The Referee, a paper which described itself as *The Unique
Sunday Journal, founded in 1877 by Pendragon!* Its contributors signed themselves with the names of The Knights of
the Round Table. The Sphinx chose to call herself 'Elaine'
and her column *White and Gold*. It is a curious fact that she
rarely enjoyed the company of women, disliking the subjects
that absorbed them – with the exception of affairs of the
heart, in which she was always interested – yet she was able
successfully to carry out her undertaking for several years.
One wonders if the readers of *White and Gold* recognised
the mockery with which the author sometimes wrote for
them. If not, what could they have made of the following
recommendation of a watering-place ? 'If your husband cannot
yet actually play golf, he can watch the links being laid out –
which I should think quite as amusing.'

These articles, of no literary value, are moving reading
for one who knew their author. In many of them she
reveals her tastes and opinions and it is like hearing them
from her own voice. For instance, she writes: 'Balzac is,
like Shakespeare, for all time. There may be fewer Eugénie
Grandets now but there are no fewer Madame Marneffes.

Mrs Cyril Martineau

W. Somerset Maugham

From a painting by Sir Gerald Kelly, KCVO, PPRA

One never tires of Jane Austen, her characters are so real and well differentiated. Henry James's characters are very real, very subtle, very delicately understood; many of them almost too full of a deep refinement and high scruples. An exception is Mrs Brook in *The Awkward Age*, who is delightfully, cynically matter-of-fact while having an almost childlike simplicity and delicious sense of humour.' Of the characters in Paul Bourget's novels, most popular in the nineteen hundreds, the Sphinx writes: 'The women are carefully analyzed psychological heroines eating out their hearts in their blue boudoirs. The "club-men" for whom they break their little hearts seem generally hardly worth it, though Monsieur Bourget himself evidently has the highest respect for them because they belong to the Jockey.'

While on the subject of the Sphinx's literary taste, it may be of interest that she loved all the novels of Dickens, particularly the picture he gives of London, for which she had an almost mystic love. Thackeray was another of her favourites, and she never forgot her first reading of *Vanity Fair*, nor indeed the joy she experienced in early youth of being gradually steeped in the works of Robert Louis Stevenson. She re-read the novels of Flaubert, Henry James and Proust continually. Of her contemporaries she loved Hardy and Meredith but had little admiration for the works of John Oliver Hobbes and Frank Danby, whose masculine names concealed the identities of Mrs Pearl Craigie and Mrs Julia Frankau. The former had succeeded the Sphinx in the affections of George Moore, and had collaborated with him in the writing of a first act of a comedy called *The Fool's Hour*, and a proverb in one act called *Journey's End in Lover's Meeting*. Anthony Hope was a favourite of the Sphinx; she particularly liked his book, the *Dolly Dialogues*, in which his flippancy appealed to her more than that of E. F. Benson.

'Elaine' divided her articles under such headings as *Conventional Conversation, The Virtues of Precious Stones, Advice to Lovers, The Art of Listening* and *Baby Parties*. Of the latter she writes: 'It is sincerely to be hoped that the new fashion of giving parties for children under four will not be generally imitated. It seems too young to be troubled with social responsibilities. One baby I know is a most genial host, and though he cannot speak yet, invites in pantomime his guests to "help themselves and pass the bottle". Others are pleasanter as guests. But five or even six is surely young enough to "come out". It seems beginning the *mondain* element rather too early in life when one has to crawl into Society on one's hands and knees because one is not yet old enough to walk.'

'Elaine' parodied the *Answers to Correspondents Column*, then appearing in another paper, although she pretended to her own readers to take it seriously. She writes: 'There is something very touching about the following avowal and in the way it is expressed; something so naïf in its complete reliance on the opinion of the Unknown and Unseen Authority: "Dear Editor, I had been going with a young man for some time when he cast me aside and went with my lady friend. Now she has cast him aside and goes with his brother. I am going with another young man at present, but the one who jilted me would very much like to come back again. I love him better than the young man I go with now. Kindly advise me whether or not I should go back to him. Shop-girl." ' *Elaine* comments on this:

'There seem to be many complications in this case. The "Lady Friend" is apparently as unreliable in the world of the "Shop-girl" as she is in all other social conditions of which I have ever heard. The Editor responds by saying that "Shop-girl" would show but little pride and dignity if she allowed herself to be picked up like a cast-off glove.

At the same time if "she feels she must" take this young man back, she should do so. Now this is all very well, but what about that other young man who was taken to fill the place of the fickle one? It seems rather hard on him. However perhaps the "Lady-Friend", who seems of such a mercurial disposition, may in time "cast off" the second brother, and, as she evidently has a fancy for the admirers of "Shop-Girl", may console the second young man.'

Later, the Sphinx wrote the following parody of a column called *Can I be of Any Use?* run at the time by Viola Tree in another newspaper: 'Question: I would like to become a— Should I have to become a— I should prefer a monastery, if possible out of England. I am an excellent climber. If I get on, could I keep up my music and dancing? Answer: Your letter is so illegible I cannot read if you wish to become a monk or a monkey. I will answer for both or either. The latter would be frightfully easy for you, keep up your climbing, nutcracking, and chattering. Just be yourself and if you pass your exam you might get into the Zoo. I see no objection to your keeping up your music and dancing. On the other hand if you wish to become a monk, – but I can't read the word, what a bore you are.'

'Elaine' gives an example of a miserable moment in her column. It concerns a somewhat touchy man who, offended with another man at his club, has written (after a dozen rough copies) a neat letter saying, 'I am bound to say I greatly resent your attitude', etc. and has posted the letter. He feels something is wrong. He looks at the dictionary; also at his rough draft. He finds he has written a dignified admirable letter, in well-chosen words, but has spelt 'apology' with two p's.

Connoisseurs of the period will enjoy the atmosphere evoked by the following episode. In 1903, long skirts were worn and it was considered attractive to hold them up when crossing the streets, and thought that the way the Parisiennes did this was inimitable; 'Elaine' tells of a South American girl who wished to do this in the right manner, and therefore wrote to certain French celebrities for advice. Sarah Bernhardt replied: 'I never hold up my dress, I like long gowns and the natural soft flowing folds they form on the ground. So you see, I cannot advise you. If I did I would say, do not hold them up, let them fall.' Réjane replied courteously, 'I am sorry I cannot tell you; I never walk, I always drive.' Polaire answered: 'How can I tell you how to hold up a skirt? I never wear anything but a short walking dress.' Jeanne Granier said with a merry laugh: 'How can I tell you? When I cross the road all I know is, I clutch hold of my dress with both hands, I don't know how, and run across.'

In the middle of the year 1905, the Sphinx ceased to write for *The Referee*. The seed planted ten years before by Grant Richards was beginning to bear fruit. She set herself and all her energies to writing a novel to be called *The Twelfth Hour*. It was published in 1907.

CHAPTER V

The Sphinx did all her writing in bed, in a confusion of foolscap, newspapers, cigarettes and oranges. A tall, gaunt stenographer would spend hours daily being dictated to, typing and generally assisting the writer, whose amiability and sense of fun seemed to make up for her impracticability. The highly-skilled secretary, who had fallen under her spell, would gladly go out to do some trivial commission in the middle of a morning's work. Miss Jackson was sparing in her display of any reaction to the Sphinx's work; with the result that bringing an unwilling smile to her secretary's rather grim face was the greatest of encouragements to the writer.

When an author is in love with a publisher it is often, as it was in this case, a spur to literary creation. The Sphinx was quite undeterred by the fact that Grant Richards was married, was later divorced and remarried. At the back of her mind was the thought, expressed by Robert Ross in a letter, that some men treated their marriages as others do a little villa in Richmond. In actual fact, Grant Richards was a devoted husband and father but, when with the Sphinx, never spoke of his domestic life. He was a most courteous, smiling, and patient man. Although in conversation a persistent splitter of infinitives, as a judge of literary talent he had no rivals. Eventually a love of good living was to be his undoing. The Sphinx was attracted by his good looks and noncommittal manner; she christened him *Tacitus*. In 1923

he wrote: 'When Mrs Leverson had expressed her wishes,
it was difficult to evade them; she willed; her friends obeyed.'
Then she was urging Grant Richards to publish the work
of the three gifted Sitwells. In 1906 it had been the other
way. It was Grant Richards who willed and she who obeyed.

Her six novels were published between 1907 and 1916.
Although there were some who agreed with Julian Leverson
that the plots were too slight, they were always well received
by the reviewers.

Frank Richardson, a handsome young barrister who
forced his way into journalism, was a new friend of the post-
Deanery Street era. He wanted the Sphinx to marry him,
but nothing would induce her to convert the amicable
separation from Ernest into the scandal of a divorce. It
cannot be said that Frank Richardson had any influence upon
her; she was, however, touched by his affection and
he became her 'escort'. Was there something in the Irish
temperament which particularly appealed to her? The three
men who had made the deepest impression upon her until
she became a great friend of Grant Richards had been Irish-
men; Desart, George Moore, and Oscar Wilde.

At Paris Plage one summer, a curious group was staying
at the same hotel. These were Colette, her husband Willy
(the nom-de-plume of the writer H. Gauthier-Villars) his
mistress Meg Villars, Marcel Boulestin, and the Marquise
de Morny, a lady who dressed like a man. Frank Richardson,
who knew Boulestin, pointed to the Marquise, who was
placidly drinking her liqueur and smoking her usual cigar,
and asked: 'Who is this old pederast?' The situation was then
explained. The only one of the group who became the Sphinx's
friend was Marcel Boulestin; she was prudish about other
women and seldom made friends with any who were thought
scandalous. At the time of the Paris-Plage meeting, Colette
and Willy's *Claudine* books were yellow-backed novels to

be hidden behind the cushions of the sofa if one was caught reading them.

In London, Max Beerbohm lived a few minutes away from Radnor Place, in Upper Berkeley Street, with his two sisters and his mother. (They had left Hyde Park Place.) Mrs Beerbohm was a tiny little lady who looked very old and as if she always must have done so; she wore skirts that trailed on the ground. Constance, the elder sister, never married. She was half-sister to Max and full sister to Beerbohm Tree. Agnes, Mrs Neville, was Max's full sister. She had prematurely grey hair and ran a dress-making establishment in Connaught Street. They, and their brother Beerbohm Tree, had a charmingly vague manner, in contrast to Max, who was very much on the spot. The Sphinx liked nothing better than visiting them and was undaunted by the piercing yaps of the idol of the family, a small Pomeranian dog. Max wrote rhymes about his pet:

> *If you have anything to ask, ask it—*
> *Where does Dandy like to bask? Basket.*

Witty, fascinating Max had an intensely cosy side to his nature. One afternoon he was going out as the Sphinx arrived, and was heard to say to his mother enviously: 'I expect you have ordered yourselves a delicious tea.' He would accompany the Sphinx and other friends to the seaside, usually to St Margaret's Bay. Once when the Sphinx's daughter was very young she was climbing up a slope in advance of her nurse with something curious and exciting to impart. Panting with excitement, she broke in on the grown-up people's conversation. They were sitting on the turf laughing and talking as usual. 'I've just seen a baby adder playing with a cat,' she announced. Silence fell for a minute; then they began to laugh loudly. The sound was disagreeable to the ears of the child, whose eyes welled with tears. 'What extraordinary things children do invent,' said

one. Her mother reproved her gently for telling 'a story'.
The child persisted: 'But it's true.' 'Nonsense' they all
said. No one believed her except Max. 'I'm sure the child
is telling the truth,' he said firmly. Sure enough, the nurse
then emerged over the crest of the slope and confirmed
the incident.

One of the sweetest-natured women that can be imagined
was Aubrey Beardsley's sister Mabel. She and the Sphinx
saw a great deal of each other after the death of Aubrey.
She was a devout Catholic; so it is a little surprising that
we learn from Yeats that she sometimes shocked him with
her improper stories. Oscar had said she resembled a daisy,
but one cannot imagine any daisy having so grotesquely
affected a manner as had Mabel. This stood in the way of the
Sphinx's daughter liking her, in spite of Mabel's generosity
in the giving of birthday and Christmas presents. Mabel
was tall, pretty, with the colouring of a sweetpea and an
ambition to be an actress; in spite of the influence of Aubrey's
old school-friend, Charles Cochran, Mabel achieved little
success in this sphere. She did however appear in 1904 in a
play called *Golden Light* with the beautiful American
actress Mrs Brown-Potter. Mabel Beardsley* was the original
of the character Miss Luscombe in the Sphinx's novel *The
Limit*. Another woman whose affected way of talking was
painful to hear was Olive Custance, known as 'Opal' after
her poem of that name; she married Lord Alfred Douglas
in 1902. Opal was a sweet romantic creature who had been
in love with Bosie since childhood. She called him 'Prince'
and herself his Page. He only made up his mind to marry her
when she became engaged to one of his friends. They eloped,
because Colonel Custance, not surprisingly, opposed the
match; Opal and Bosie lived happily together for a few

* Yeats wrote many poems to her, some unpublished. Max Beerbohm said
he couldn't overstate her strange charm. She died in 1913.

years, and separately, in friendship, until her death in 1904.

The Sphinx's favourite woman friend after the death of Kitty Martineau, was her youngest sister Violet, whose qualities as a confidante were unsurpassed. She was twelve years younger than the Sphinx, very intuitive and sympathetic and knew instinctively that most people require an audience to their lives. Violet had many suitors, one of whom was Sir Arthur Sullivan, who in his old age fell in love with her and asked her to marry him. He was refused.

Violet shared her eldest sister's love of the works of Henry James and her enjoyment in the study of human nature, so they had plenty to talk about; she also shared her sister Sybil's fondness for music; when Violet married Sydney Schiff, better known as the writer Stephen Hudson, her sisters almost resented that she was no longer available to them at all hours of the day. It was an idyllic marriage. Her genius for friendship found a wide range to express itself. Marcel Proust, Katharine Mansfield and T. S. Eliot became her close friends, and artists and musicians have always sought the special pleasure of her company. Perhaps it was because her character was exceptionally well-balanced that, as she grew older, more and more people came to her either for inspiration, consolation or advice.

The Sphinx was fond of her mother but far more so of her father, for whom she had a profound respect. It humiliated her that her money troubles caused him anxiety. So much did this prey upon her mind that she developed a Cordelia fantasy, thinking that when her pretty, prosperous sisters clustered round him they were belittling her and her talent. She once said: 'If only Papa knew, I am the only one of the family whose name will live.' He died at the beginning of the First World War. Until then, the words 'Don't tell Papa' were frequently on her lips.

Ernest came back to England from Canada once or twice

on a brief visit. Each time he would upset the little household by finding fault with everything. Conversations such
as those between the characters Bruce and Edith in three
of the Sphinx's novels would occur:

'It is awful not having a valet,' said Bruce.

'It would be more awful if we had one. Where would he
go? In the bathroom?'

Then Bruce would say, 'I have large ideas, I own it. It's
difficult for me to be petty about trifles.'

Ernest, like Bruce, would appear to help his wife by
making a budget of her expenses. Once having done that,
he considered the matter settled and the bills paid, and would
return to Canada.

The purely frivolous element in the Sphinx's life at that
time was supplied by Cosmo Gordon-Lennox. He bubbled
over with gaiety, charm and good nature, wrote plays and
sometimes appeared on the stage himself. It was from him
that the character of Harry Defreyne in her novel *The
Limit* was derived. He married the actress Marie Tempest
with disastrous results to him. Whatever his faults may
have been, and his wife discovered that these included at
least one of Oscar Wilde's, he was a man it was impossible
not to like when in his company. He had the gift of making
life fun. He did not lack kindness or courage either, and
won admiration for both during the First World War. He
died soon after the Armistice.

On December 17, 1908, eight years after Oscar Wilde's
death, a dinner was given at the Ritz Hotel in honour of
Robert Ross, who had succeeded in winding up Wilde's
estate. The guests numbered nearly three hundred, and were
headed by the Prime Minister. Robert Ross made an
informative speech, making the announcement that he had
received a gift of £2,000, on the condition that the giver
should be anonymous, to place a suitable monument to Oscar

Wilde at Père-Lachaise and that this work should be carried out by the brilliant young sculptor, Mr Jacob Epstein. The speech ended with these words: 'May I take that generous gift and your hospitality this evening as symbols that in after years it will be my privilege to boast that I was the occasion, though never the cause, of giving back to Oscar Wilde's children the laurels of their distinguished father untarnished save by tears.'

Earlier in that year Ada had made the acquaintance of Oscar Wilde's son Vyvyan, who was then twenty-two. His personality appealed very much to her; she found it fun to be with him as they laughed at the same things. Years later, in his autobiography,* he records in generous words the impression she first made upon him and how her influence affected his life: 'Another lady with whom I became great friends was Mrs Ada Leverson whom my father called the Gilded Sphinx of Golden Memory. She was still very beautiful with the aureole of gold tinted hair from which she derived the name my father had given her.' Vyvyan goes on to say that it was through her and Oscar Wilde's great friend Miss Schuster, that he obtained a new outlook on life and on human nature, a broadening of views and the breakdown of prejudices and inhibitions.

*   *   *

When alone with her daughter, the Sphinx would suggest some game to play. At meals they would pretend to be at a restaurant and discuss imaginary people at another table. These games were played as much for the amusement of the mother as for the child. Sometimes one of them would exclaim: 'I've thought of someone!' – a cue for the other to ask the usual questions: Dark or Fair? Man or Woman? Nice or Nasty? Strangely enough, the answers always built up

* *Son of Oscar Wilde*, published by Rupert Hart-Davis in 1956.

a desirable person. (Do I really know a rich, fair, young, handsome, unmarried man living in the country?) If in the end the person guessed turned out to be someone they saw continually and took for granted, he would be more appreciated in the future. When there were others present, the game of Sonnets might be played, or Consequences. Detailed accounts of parties and visits were always welcome. Once, after lunching with the wife of a Leverson uncle, the daughter complained that she had not enjoyed it. Asked why, she explained: 'Because Aunt Gerda said when I dropped a spoon: "That isn't very good for Rose's silver, is it Rose?" to the parlourmaid.' Was it the note of hypocritical patronage in the remark that offended? In any case, to the daughter's surprise her mother was delighted with the observation. Having had the experience of being married to a husband with an uncertain temper, the Sphinx would often impress upon her daughter that nothing is so important to the happiness of people as the temper of those with whom they live; that the next-best thing to a sweet-tempered companion is one who sulks. While your companion is sulking, she would say, you can continue your own occupation or train of thought; you can read or write, completely undisturbed by bitter sarcastic remarks or open abuse; and when the sulking has worn itself out you can resume amicable relations!

*   *   *

When the Sphinx met William Somerset Maugham for the first time she was already an enthusiastic admirer of his novel *Liza of Lambeth*. (Later, when he produced *Of Human Bondage*, she considered it to be his masterpiece.) She was amazed at the talents of the shy, dark-eyed, good-looking young man. When he had two or three plays being acted simultaneously in London, she could not help but be reminded of Oscar Wilde's similar achievement. Willie Maugham admitted in a letter that he did not know how to spell the word Sphinx. His decision to do so with a 'y' gives his letters to her an added distinction. His visits were looked forward to eagerly and a large photograph of him became part of her personal surroundings.

As she grew older, the Sphinx became possessive in her friendships and even a little ruthless in her efforts to see as much as possible of the people she liked. In his *Noble Essences*, Osbert Sitwell, who knew her later, describes her nature in this respect: 'Quite sure of herself, she did not in the least mind what impression people in whom she took no interest formed of her, she paid no attention to bores and those whom she thought stupid, unless for some reason or other they, in their very folly, amused her. She craved passionately, however, the good opinion, and the society of those whom she liked.'

Evelyn had married, as her second husband, Walter Behrens, President of the Chamber of Commerce in Paris, where she made her home. When staying in London at Claridge's Hotel, Ada's daughter saw her aunt for the first time. So charming and extraordinarily appealing was Evelyn's appearance and whole personality that her niece could not rest until she had brought about a reconciliation between her and her mother. Had this aim not been achieved, the shadow over Ada's life caused by Evelyn's death soon after this meeting would have been an even darker one.

Fancy-dress balls were extremely popular in the years which led up to the First World War. Diaghileff's Russian Ballet revolutionized English taste. The Sphinx, however, was happiest when, dressed soberly in a masque and domino, she would attend one of these balls, accompanied by a gay young party. Russian national dress was a favourite disguise. People took meticulous trouble about their costumes although, as the Sphinx observed, no one at the ball was

interested in any fancy-dress but his or her own. The Albert Hall
on New Year's Eve smelt of an indescribably exciting mixture
of grease-paint, scent and sweat. The Sphinx seldom missed a
performance of the Russian ballet and applauded Nijinsky and
Karsarvina with the other balletomanes of the time.

When the war broke out it affected the Sphinx as it did
many other middle-aged women. She took up minor work
for the Red Cross and helped in the allocation of Belgian
refugees. There were one brother, several nephews and
many friends about whom to be anxious.

*   *   *

In 1916, *Love at Second Sight*, the Sphinx's sixth and last
novel, was published; Robert Ross wrote of it thus: 'Although
I am really so unhappy and horribly unwell and generally
tedious (how 1890 the word tedious is!), I have been able to
delight in *Love at Second Sight*. I feel very like Bruce [a
character in the book], 'a malade imaginaire', but the war
keeps *me* alive, is in fact the only thing that does, besides
your book. I don't think, however, I can ever forgive you
for throwing away Frabelle – you must write another book
about her and mention how she missed the boat at Liverpool
and wasn't allowed to sail with Bruce. She is a really great
impressionist picture by Whistler or Manet (and, to tell you a
secret, rather dumps the others, dear Sphinx). Lady Conroy
is one of your superb miniatures – Pre-Raphaelite in truth
and observation.

Ever your affectionate

Robbie.

I suppose you have seen D's [Alfred Douglas] book about
me, or rather pamphlet.'

Little is known of the Sphinx's friendship with the American
writer Theodore Dreiser, how they met and how much they

saw of each other. The following letter appears to have been
written soon after their first meeting:

> Normandy Hotel,
> 7 Rue de L'Echelle,
> Paris.
> Jan 15, 1912

Dear Mrs Leverson,
   I was very pleased to hear from you and to get your book,
which I promise to read at the earliest possible opportunity . . .
It is very beautiful here, gay and immoral, but I speak no
French and so am handicapped. I'm sorry you're not coming.
However, I knew quite well it couldn't be at the time I
spoke – not in likelihood. I'm so glad you like my book so
much and that you like me. I know we shall get on and I
value my friendships most highly.

   Their mutual friend, Grant Richards, was to save Dreiser's
life by deterring him from sailing to America from England in
the *Titanic*.
   One of the Sphinx's marked characteristics was her
understanding of schoolboys. All boys who knew her would
seek her company whenever possible. Her attitude to life
appealed to them, and theirs to her. Whether her companion
was an ordinary, manly boy whose main interest was sport,
or a talented precocious future aesthete, it was the same.
They would be sure to get on with her like a house on fire.
Often she would be seen at luncheon with a nephew, or the
son of a friend, both at their ease, perhaps engrossed in
their respective books while eating, occasionally exchanging
ideas. There was no hint of patronage in her manner to
them. They talked to one another as intelligent grown-up
people do. She felt no impulse, as with her daughter, to play
imaginative games with them, they were so much at their

ease. This understanding of boys and very young men was
put to good account in her stories in *The Yellow Book* and
in two of her novels, as for instance in the short dialogue in
her first novel, *The Twelfth Hour*, between the sixteen-year-
old Savile and his aunt:

' "I shall have to be going now, Aunt William, got an
appointment."

"With whom, my dear?"

"Yes," said Savile dryly. He did not approve of the direct
method of ascertaining what one wants to know. He would
confide, but never answered questions." '

Again, in *Bird of Paradise*, the truth of her portrait of one
type of twelve-year-old boy is striking. Clifford is conversing
with his elderly mother.

She asks: ' "Tell me something about your life at school,
darling."

' "How do you mean?"

' "Well, haven't you any nice little friends at school,
Clifford, any favourites?"

'He smiled. "Oh, good Lord, Mother, of course I haven't.
People don't have little friends. I don't know what you
mean."

'She looked rather pained. "No friends? Oh dear, dear,
dear. But are there no nice boys that you like?"

' "No, most of them are awful rotters."

'She put down her beads. "Clifford! I am shocked to hear
this. Rotters! I suppose that is one of your school expressions.
Poor little fellow. I shall make a note of that."

'He looked up rather frightened. "What on earth for?"

' "Why, I shall certainly speak to your Master about it.
Oh! To think that you haven't got a single friend in the
school. All bad boys. There must be something wrong
somewhere."

(Then, to reassure his mother, Clifford admits):

Oscar Wilde

Osbert Sitwell

' "There's one chap who's fairly decent, a chap called Pickering."

' "To think there should be only one boy fairly decent in all that enormous school!"

' "Oh well! He's simply *frightfully* decent, as a matter of fact. Pickering fairly takes it. He's top-hole. There's nothing he can't do."

' "What does he do, darling?"

"Ah! I can't exactly explain. He's a bit of all right. It's frightfully smart to be seen with him."

' "Clifford – really! I'd no idea you had these social views. Of course, you're quite right dear. I've always been in favour of your being friends with little gentlemen, but I shouldn't like you to be at all what is called a snob."

'Clifford laughed. "I never said Pickering was a gentleman, big or little! You don't understand, Mother. I mean it's smart to be seen with him because – oh, I can't explain. He's all right."

' "Would you like, dear, to have this young Master Pickering to tea here one day?"

'He looked up and around the room. "Oh, no, Mother. I shouldn't care for him to come here."

' "Why not, dear?"

' "Oh, I can't explain exactly; it isn't the sort of place for him."

'Lady Kellynch was positively frightened to ask why, for fear her boy should show contempt for his own home, so she didn't go into the matter, but remarked: "I should think a beautiful house in Onslow Square, with a garden like this, was just the thing for a boy to like."

'He shook his head with a humorous expression of contempt. "Pickering wouldn't go into a *square* garden, Mother."

'She waited a moment, wondering what shaped garden

was suited to him, what form of pleasaunce was worthy of the presence of this exceptional boy . . .'

The author's fondness and understanding of the very young male would have made her the ideal mother of sons. It will be seen later that one young man whom she captivated when a schoolboy became important in her life as an adult friend. Of her four brothers, from whom some of her knowledge of boys was derived, there were only two survivors; Frank, an athlete whose ambition it was to win the Diamond Sculls, who would laugh sardonically at his wife for begging him not to overtire himself whenever he went off to practice for that strenuous feat, and Charley, who had an ironic wit.

One of the Sphinx's greatest wishes was to know Henry James. For some reason the only person who was willing to bring about a meeting was Joscelyn Persse, a handsome man of leisure who spent most of his time with a married couple, former neighbours of the Leversons in Deanery Street, called Mr and Mrs Black. Arrangements for the meeting were discussed for months before it took place. When, at last, the Sphinx found herself sitting next to the great novelist, she spoke to him of his books. Something in the way she did so must have struck him, as, turning to her, he said: 'Can it be – it must be – that you are the embodiment of the incorporeal, that elusive yet ineluctable being to whom through the generations novelists have so unavoidably made invocation, in short, the Gentle Reader. I have wondered in what guise you would appear and, as it were, what incarnation you would assume.'*

It was in 1917 that the Sphinx first had the idea of writing on Oscar Wilde. Heinemann must have offered to publish what she wrote. The following letter from Robert Ross,

* *Noble Essences*, Osbert Sitwell, Macmillan, 1950.

written from the Carfax Gallery (which, incidentally, no longer belonged to him), is interesting but enigmatic:

Carfax and C. Lond.   17 Ryder Street,
                                    St James', SW.
                                    May 20, 1917

. . . It would be a great pleasure for me to see or read anything you wrote about Oscar and it would have been a real pleasure to him to think that you were doing so. Again, though I do not think I would be of much assistance, I certainly would be delighted to give it to you for what it was worth, *but* I cannot do so if Heinemann is the publisher. He has behaved very badly to me quite recently in a trade matter. I fear that I would throw every possible difficulty in the way of his publishing anything at all. The copyright of Oscar's letters (unpublished) belongs to me and I would apply for an injunction to restrain publication if any letters were printed.* There is *nothing* private in this at all and I shall be glad if you tell Heinemann next time you see him *and the reason.*

Oscar is of course public property – only his grave, his body and his letters belong to me, and Heinemann shall certainly not have anything out of them while I am alive.

If you will select a straightforward publisher who can answer business questions in an ordinary way, I shall be glad to give you any and every assistance; but I dislike *homeopathics* either in chemistry or publishers. I suppose it must be Heinemann's portrait by Rodin which one sees in decayed chemist shops?

Robert Ross never saw the essay printed. His death, at the age of forty-nine in 1918, was hastened by Alfred Douglas's

---

* The copyright has since expired, hence Rupert Hart-Davis's publication of the letters of Oscar Wilde in 1962.

persecution of him. Oscar had been right in saying that Ross's was the tragedy of the hybrid – the Pagan-Catholic. Had he not had a pagan side to his noble, unselfish character, Bosie could not have threatened and attacked him as he did.

The Sphinx felt the loss of this friend so profoundly that it caused her to become seriously ill. Fifteen months later, when restored to health, she met Osbert Sitwell at the house of her sister Violet. He was then twenty-eight and she fifty-seven; this meeting led to an association which illuminated the rest of her life. She adopted him, as it were, in a friendship which was as dear to her as love. It is not difficult to understand the impact his personality made upon her. His original mind, his wit expressed in an infinitely attractive voice and manner, were not by any means his only attributes; she recognised immediately a solid base of kindness beneath the exterior charm.

It must be said that the Sphinx was remarkable in her relationships with men. She had known lovers, but was also able to feel a love for a man, purely platonic in its nature, which had in it a kind of hero-worship. It is doubtful if at any time of her grown-up life she was without one or the other of these emotions.

CHAPTER VI

Osbert Sitwell remembered seeing Ada Leverson for the first time when he was a schoolboy, at a restaurant. He described her as being then a youngish, elegant, golden-haired woman with a face of striking pallor, who took her place at a table in the centre of the room with an abstracted air about her. Thirteen or fourteen years later, when he saw her again, she had greatly changed in appearance. The reason for this was that, no longer being able to afford the best dress-makers nor a ladies' maid, she had simplified her way of dressing, believing that a woman after the age of fifty, who has lost her figure, should disguise the fact. Not for her the stringy neck or bulging arms of those who must wear the latest fashion at all costs. Dark loose dresses were her choice, worn high at the neck, brightened by a coloured scarf or beads. The effect was ageing but not ugly. In the daytime she would wear a large mushroom hat and in the evening her fair hair would be worn curled over her head.

The Sphinx was quick to recognise the gifts of the remark-able Sitwell trio, Edith, Osbert and Sacheverell. From the moment of her first meeting with Osbert, they and their friends became the chief interest in her life. Because of the daring of their work, they were meeting opposition on all sides. The Sitwells demanded, quite rightly, absolute loyalty; the Sphinx was capable of the fiercest of partisanship, which naturally added to the warmth of the friendship. Her encouragement, so Osbert says, helped him to persevere as a writer. At first she had not been sure if he were wise to abandon the idea of fighting a Parliamentary election; but directly he read his first prose to her, a story called 'The Machine Breaks Down', referred to earlier, she said to him, 'I feel happy now; you were right to give up Scarborough'.

Friendship with writers stimulated the Sphinx's own creative instinct; it had done so many years earlier, after her meeting with Oscar Wilde. She wrote and published in a literary magazine a story called *The Blow*. It is different from any of her former work. The following letter refers to it:

Sunday night.   Marlborough Club,
                                                               Pall Mall, SW1.

My dear Sphinx (or is that too familiar?)

It is only the horror of my handwriting that has prevented my writing to you 'ere now.

Ever so many thanks for the two copies of the *English Review*, which I read last night with the greatest enjoyment. I look forward so much to your next article.

In case this letter falls into enemy hands, let me say how lucky you are in having no parents to open your letters and comment on them, as mine would do if I ever received any!

I have spent a painful day, circling St Paul's in a motor omnibus; and now I rest calmly in this [word illegible] listening to the sonorous breathing of the venerable Lord Chaplin, who is slowly sinking into deserved repose.

Do come and see us again soon. On Wed. night I go to a party at Lady Rothermere's – at least I hope it will be a party, tho' last time I went only two or three were gathered together. Will you be there?

                    Yours ever,
                                         Osbert Sitwell.

Ada loved Edith Sitwell and her poems. Before one reading of these, she sent the poetess a laurel wreath to crown her. It was worn and both the giver and the garlanded hoped the emblem would 'put the audience in their place', as it were. Both adoring Osbert, they were miserable and wretched before his first visit to America. No matter that it was only for six weeks and not months, as they told each other, they neither of them could settle down to work properly with this parting hanging over them.

*   *   *

With a sense of buoyancy the Sphinx left Radnor Place to live in a flat in South Audley Street, happy to be near to the house she had so loved. This final phase of her life brought a new pleasure: travel in the exciting company of the Sitwell brothers and William Walton, then at the start of his musical career. They would visit Sicily and Italy, see Max Beerbohm and his wife at Rapallo, and stay at Amalfi in a hotel which had once been a monastery. A stalwart porter would carry the Sphinx up the steep incline from the street; in those days the massive lift had not been installed. In spring and autumn she would be found in Florence, surrounded by new acquaintances and old friends, such as Reggie Turner, Norman Douglas, Pino Orioli and Richard Aldington. Sometimes Ronald Firbank would arrive at her hotel to visit her, generally bearing a large bouquet. The young Sitwells would come down from Montegufoni, their neighbouring castle, and all would drink coffee and eat ices at Doney's. Whereas Lady Ida, their mother, became her friend, Sir George Sitwell did not appreciate the Sphinx, nor she him. Osbert tells how, when his father moved from the hotel in London in which he usually stayed, to Batt's Hotel in Dover Street, the Sphinx observed: 'I hear your father's changed belfries!'

In London once again the young Sitwells would take their friend on expeditions to Hampton Court and Greenwich. Once,when asked what were her arrangements for the early summer, she replied that one of them was coming to tea that afternoon. This was Harold Acton, who had made her acquaintance in Florence while on long leave from Eton, when he discovered her to be a kindred spirit.

Accompanied by the brilliant nineteen-year-old Harold, the Sphinx went to the Aeolian Hall in June 1923, to see the first performance of *Façade*, of which the authors were the three Sitwells and the composer, William Walton. There was no one visible on the stage during the performance. 'I would like to have seen more real people in the audience,' complained Harold. 'I thought there *were* more,' she observed in a tone of surprise, 'you brought more – surely you did?' This was the Sphinx at her airiest, remarks Harold Acton, who quotes this small exchange in his *The Memoirs of an Aesthete**. The audience was in part hostile and the critics ferocious. The performance caused a furore and the authors were obliged to go about as if they had committed a murder.

The year 1923 was an important one to the Sphinx; Grant Richards was persuaded to publish Sacheverell Sitwell's prose work, *Southern Baroque Art*, and Osbert's book of poems, *Out of the Flame*. It was a pity that Grant Richards went bankrupt after having sold one of Osbert's books to two different publishers, having gone to Paris for a spree on the proceeds, leaving the two publishers to fight it out. Another author who owed publication of his work by Grant Richards to the Sphinx's powers of persuasion, was Sir Coleridge Kennard. He was the son of Helen Kennard, who became Mrs James Carew, the generous lady who provided the money for Epstein's statue for Oscar Wilde's tomb, helped financially by the Sphinx's brother-in-law, Sydney Schiff. Coleridge Kennard, in his middle

* Methuen, 1948.

thirties at the time of the book's publication, was a distinguished diplomat; before his marriage he was known to have
had a romantic attachment with a married woman. He never
became celebrated as a writer but his work was considered
promising by Max Beerbohm and Harold Nicolson.

In 1922 news had been received that Ernest had died
suddenly in Canada. Like his father, he lost his life in the
midst of enjoying it. While standing in the frosty sunshiny
air taking leave of friends with whom he had been having
Christmas lunch, he fell to the ground with a heart attack.
Excepting for this sad news, nothing but pleasant things
occurred in the Sphinx's life from then on. The event that
caused happiness to all concerned was the marriage of her
daughter to Guy Wyndham, as his second wife. His son by
his first wife, Dick Wyndham, was a great friend of Sacheverell
Sitwell. The dinner-party before the wedding in the South
Audley Street flat included Guy Wyndham, his son and his
daughter Olivia, Osbert Sitwell and Max Beerbohm. The
birth of two grandsons in the next few years helped to heal
the wound which was always in the Sphinx's heart since the
early death of her own son, George.

In July 1923, soon after the wedding, Ada wrote to
George Moore about his forthcoming play. Her letter
was well-timed. He had been rebuking his great friend
Lady Cunard for her neglect of him.* It would appear by
his reply to Ada that his thoughts had gladly gone back
to his warm friendship with her of thirty-two years past.

121 Ebury Street.
I was glad to get your letter, dear Ada, for I often think
of you. I am glad too that you wish to see *The Coming of
Gabrielle* and I will guarantee the comedy to be as pretty as

---

* George Moore: *Letters, 1895-1933 to Lady Cunard*, pp. 126-7, Hart-
Davis, 1957.

the title. If a man cannot express himself in the title he is
not likely to express himself in the book or play. I was told
today that the tickets I asked for would be sent to me tomorrow Saturday, so will you come to tea on Sunday at
half-past four and I'll give you one and a kiss in memory of
the kisses of yesteryear?

Always yours,

George Moore.

The meeting cannot have been altogether a success,
according to the following letter written the day after it.

121 Ebury Street
Monday night.

My dear Ada,

You are welcome to the second ticket, no lady more so.
Please make use of it and if you cannot find a companion
at the last hour, hand it to the man at the box office, who will
sell it, if he can.

I look forward to seeing you again. Now that we have
broken the ice, we shall be at ease and have more to say. It
will be better next time.

Affectionately yours,

George Moore.

The following extracts, quoted from Osbert Sitwell's
letters, serve to show the liveliness of their friendship. He
tells her of an article in the *Daily Mail* about a murder that
had been committed at Bournemouth. 'It said that robbery
is ruled out as a motive, and that, therefore, apart from the
brutality of it, the murder had an unpleasant, unEnglish
appearance ! ! !' There are in the following letters what
must be the first references to 'Ginger', the name given to
their father by the three young Sitwells. These should interest

the many admirers of Sir Osbert Sitwell's autobiography. In his study of Sir George Sitwell, the author has created one of the most extraordinary and amusing characters in English literature.

From the Grand Hotel, Cap d'Ail, Osbert writes: '. . . Have you seen "Ginger" or anyone? "G." writes to me that he "is troubled with a nervous movement of the muscles behind the ears." It sounds awful.'

Hotel Capuccini Convent, Amalfi

Last year in the summer, do you remember that Edith had a row with a General in the *Daily Mail?* The General wrote to it, saying it was obvious from her photograph that she was a person of low mentality.

The latest news is that the General has been arrested for being drunk and disorderly . . . in Cambridge Circus! ! He danced, sang and then became unconscious!

Edith at once wrote to him in these terms:

'Dear Sir Reginald,

I want to be the first to congratulate you on having woken to find yourself famous!'

Best love,

Osbert.

From the Castle of Montegufoni, Osbert again writes: 'Dearest Sphinx, "Ginger" has taken to using fearful language and is always shouting *"Will* you keep your mouth shut?" So inappropriate I think . . .' From the Hotel Royal, Dieppe: ' "Ginger" is trying to frighten me about money. "Soon," he said, "I fear that the bailiffs will be in again." I told him not to worry about it, and added that I never went to sleep without looking under the bed to see if a bailiff were there! He is rather pleased with *Triple Fugue* and says there may be money in it. But not for him! ! . . . ' Again from

Montegufoni, Osbert writes: '. . . *Façade* was a great
success and Willie* has been referred to in one paper as "il"
world-famous wanton! . . .' Later, '. . . Rome is gay, and
much less eternal than it used to be, at least I think so. I've
nearly finished my novel – hope you will like it. Do send me
a line. *A* line! . . .' [The Sphinx was inclined to write long
letters in handwriting which, alas, had become difficult to
decipher.] In an undated letter from Dresden Osbert writes:

'Berlin is too terrible for words, the whole scene laid for
some appalling catastrophe which can't be far off. It costs the
Germans £36 to get a pair of shoes re-soled. All the middle
classes are absolutely starving. I went to see Max Meyer-
feld; the translator of Wilde's books and a great friend of
Robbie. I suspect he is near starvation himself. It is really
ghastly! And all the hotels are full of guzzling foreigners,
stuffing themselves with food . . .'

From Woodend:
'. . . Both Mother and Father are very tiresome. The
former very tearful about the Royal Family and especially
about the Prince of Wales. She cried to me about it at
dinner on Friday night saying, "They say the poor boy has
to have a bottle of champagne every night . . . no one will
ever know what that boy got through . . ." but whether she
referred to India or champagne, I couldn't find out . . .'

In one letter which made the Sphinx very happy indeed,
Osbert told her that to have such a friend as she was a
comfort to all three of them – that she was unanimously
adopted as a member of the family. And in another, after she
had left them in Florence, she was deeply flattered to be
told . . . 'I hope to see you in a week. I can never tell you
how glad we are that you came abroad with us. In addition
to all your other attributes, you are a marvellous traveller . . .'

* Now Sir William Walton.

Sun. Renishaw.

Dearest Sphinx,

. . . I am collecting my satires and poems for a book –
I don't dedicate the whole book to you – because Sachie has
already done it, but will you, out of your great sweetness,
choose a poem to which I may attach your name?

"Ginger" announces that he has found out that, if
suffering from insomnia, you can go to sleep by lying in 13
different positions, and his discovery he is shortly giving to
the world, in a suitably illustrated small volume, entitled:

Thirteen Postures
by
Sir George R. Sitwell.

It should be quite a collector's piece, shouldn't it?

*   *   *

In 1925, the Sphinx wrote to T. S. Eliot, then editor of the
Criterion, and offered to write an essay on Wilde for the
quarterly, a short story and an essay on Proust. In replying,
Mr Eliot wrote: '. . . I should like to have the Wilde as soon
as possible. I am very pleased to hear about the *Consultation*
too [This was the title of the short story]. I have been
thinking about the Proust too. But in April or July, as it
happens, we are having something by Proust and several
things about Proust and I don't think we can publish any
more for a long time after that . . . I like the title very much –
The Importance. [The Sphinx intended calling her essay
'The Importance of being Oscar'.]

The essay on Wilde was published in January 1926, under
the title, *The Last First Night*. Other contributors to the
Criterion included Jean Cocteau, D. H. Lawrence, Virginia
Woolf and Aldous Huxley, to name only a few famous
names, so it was as great an honour to be writing for this
quarterly in 1926 as for *The Yellow Book* thirty years earlier.

CHAPTER VII

Harold Acton was staying at the seaside with his brother, William, who was recovering from an accident, when he wrote the following:

April 1st 1926   Queen's Hotel,
                                                        Hastings.

It was charming of you to write me. William had what others besides the newspapers call a miraculous recovery . . . The worst troubles are over now but he is somewhat sad that the doctors forbid him henceforth 'to twine vineleaves in his hair!' Perhaps it is as well, and Hastings is more than a mere purgatory (I shall refrain, dear Sphinx, from more forceful language) . . . I hope to sojourn in London for a few days. May I pay you a visit? The Easter trippers here are incredible, and I have had quite enough of concertina-music, which I used to enjoy once upon a time, in a poem or two of Edith's. I had been meaning to write to you for some time to tell you how I enjoyed *The Last First Night:* it was quite perfect, a wonderful piece of atmospheric conjuring! I distributed copies of the *Criterion* among all my friends . . . I wish you would tell us more about Oscar . . .

The Sphinx lost no time in warning Harold that to marry at Hastings would be to repent at St Leonard's.

While visiting Sir Coleridge Kennard, known as 'Roy' to his

friends, in the south of France, the Sphinx wrote to Harold
Acton: 'Thank Heaven! I have recovered; I return to
Florence tomorrow arriving at the rather ghastly hour of
seven in the morning (if the snow permits). It would have
been such fun if only I'd not caught this cursed influenza . . .
I don't like the Riviera as I do Italy . . . Roy's wife is very
nice but hasn't half the dash and charm and liveliness of
Georgia.* Roy has been very angelic to me and I feel
grateful to them for their great kindness during my horrid
and boring indisposition. He is driving me in a hundred-
miles-an-hour Isotta to Nice tomorrow.' Although over sixty,
the Sphinx liked nothing better than being driven in a fast
car. Fear was absent from her nature.

'Isn't it awful about Diaghileff?' she wrote later to Harold;
'Will London now become Presbyterian and provincial
without their ballet? But surely someone will be found to
lead it.' It was the Sphinx who re-christened a famous Russian
dancer 'Serge Fig-leafer'.

In July 1930, Harold Acton received a letter from Reggie
Turner, an old friend of his and Ada's.

Hotel Meurice, Lausanne.

The Sphinx keeps writing to me about Wyndham Lewis's
The Apes of God and I have read one or two reviews of it by
which I judge it is a disagreeable book. What do you think
of it? The Sphinx is pleased, I can see, not unnaturally,
because she is in it, but I shall never have a glimpse – nor
do I want to – of a book which costs three guineas – except
Norman Douglas's *Capri*. Do send me an account of yourself,
Willie, and the Sphinx. [Most of the originals of the
characters in Wyndham Lewis' novel were indignant at their
representation. The Sphinx was wise enough not to take it
literally and was merely amused, though also a little startled.]

* Mrs Sacheverell Sitwell.

In London there was a party given by Raymond Mortimer in Vanessa Bell's house and tea with the Hon. Mrs Henry McLaren. Sometimes the Sphinx would go to a night-club accompanied by one or two of the Bright Young People. Of these events she would write in her letters to Harold Acton.

In February 1930, the essay on Wilde was added to a small collection of his letters which was published in book form in a limited edition.* It was preceded by an introduction written by Robert Ross many years previously. Among the letters received by the Sphinx from Wilde's friends at that time, one or two survive.

William Rothenstein wrote from Max Beerbohm's Villino Chiaro at Rapallo:

My dear friend,

I read your book, so gracefully and thoughtfully written, with interest and pleasure. And I thought, too, how generous you were. Thanks for letting me read it. We left in haste, early, as Sir Oliver Lodge wanted to see Prato Pistoria and Lucca on the way back to Spezia and I had no time to send your book back. I left it with the manager of the Hotel Albione – perhaps you won't mind, when you are passing, calling for it. It was a pleasure to see you again and to find you so unchanged. I am here on my way back to London. Max is wonderfully well; he expands and glows under an Italian sky . . .

All who knew, or knew about, Alfred Douglas in the old days, feared what he would do and say. Each time anything about Wilde was written it would be followed by an avalanche of letters of indignation and abuse from Bosie. It was his conviction that he had been cruelly slandered ever since

* *Letters to the Sphinx from Oscar Wilde*, Duckworth, 1930.

Wilde's downfall, and that Robert Ross was the cause and therefore his arch-enemy. As Ross had written the preface to this latest book it was thought that Bosie would take the publication of it in bad part. Strangely enough, he did quite the contrary. At last, in the letters from Oscar, Bosie saw himself revealed to the world nearly, but not quite, as he wished. In the following to the Sphinx's daughter, he reveals once more the emotions that he had displayed for the last thirty years.

Nov. 21 – 1932

My dear Violet,

Many thanks for sending the Sphinx's book which arrived this morning . . . I am going to London on Wednesday to stay with Olive,* who now has a house at 44 Drayton Gardens, and I will take the book as I know she will want to see it. It brought back many poignant memories of old days and dear Oscar. I wish I had known the Sphinx was going to publish it. I would have asked her to let me do an introduction. Ross is like himself, insincere and 'showing off' and never quite telling the truth about anything. I think the Sphinx ought to bring out another edition and make plain all the references to me and my devotion to Oscar, and how I went to see him or wrote to him every day while he was in Holloway, all of which owing to the treachery and lies of Ross has been misrepresented all over the world for years. So that for many years I was accused by nearly everyone of having 'deserted' Oscar and 'left him to starve in Paris', when in reality I sacrificed everything and all my prospects in life by sticking to him, as I did right down to the day of his death. I have put all this in my autobiography, but the Sphinx's book ought to be more known and understood. Not one person in a thousand would guess that

* Lady Alfred Douglas.

'Jonquil', 'Fleur-de-lys' and the person whose letters he so
anxiously awaited from Rouen were all me. I *must* see the
Sphinx when she gets back, and talk to her about all this.
What an artist she is! In a few lines she has succeeded in
creating a perfect impression of Oscar which no one else
has ever succeeded in doing. Like Baudelaire she may say:
Je sais l'art d'évoquer les minutes heureuses.

> Yours affectionately,
>
> Bosie.

Giving to the world her impressions of Oscar Wilde which
were appreciated by his friends was the fulfilment of a
wish which had long been near to her heart. It can be said
that it brought her contentment.

*   *   *

In 1931 the Sphinx was pleased to receive the following
letter from Harold Acton: 'I glimpsed Tchelitchef strolling
among the Degases in the Louvre. He was with a cadaverous
fair-haired friend, and said that "Edith, [Sitwell] la pauvre,
est grippée" here in Paris. "The Hon. Arthur Vane, known
as Daisy"* is superb! I long to read it. There is nothing to
read at the moment. I seldom open a book . . . I have spent
evenings in a favourite haunt in Montparnasse, the "Boule
Blanche"; music and dancers from Martinique, and all much
livelier than the American variety (I am fed up with those
eternal blues) . . . I have no London news; the sole paper I
see is the *New York Herald*; always funny.'

*   *   *

Although in the last decade of her life deafness hampered
the Sphinx in the enjoyment of conversation, in her case

* A character in Ada Leverson's play (which was never produced), *The
Triflers.*

this was neither sad nor tiresome. She treated mis-hearing a word as a joke, and shook with silent laughter whenever it happened. The affliction did not cause her to speak loudly nor in a toneless voice: 'Gentleness was one of the qualities which distinguished her among her other more glittering characteristics', wrote Osbert Sitwell, and her voice was never otherwise. Her distaste for the company of bores which has frequently been remarked was not from intolerance or unkindness. She was in fact the embodiment of kindness and generosity. Bores are nearly always egotists, boastful and insensitive to the feelings of others. People of that kind could exhaust the Sphinx to the point of illness. Others whom she found devitalizing were those often well-meaning people who find fault with the age in which they live, and spend most of their leisure in endeavouring to prove that all things change for the worse as time goes on. One of the benefits she conferred on her friends was her infectious optimism; like Bernard Fontenelle, she never repeated horrors, believing that it is better when possible to avoid disturbing thoughts. Her gift of being completely natural won her friends in all walks of life. One of her most devoted was Mrs Alice Wardlaw, who visited her constantly at the South Audley flat and later at the Washington Hotel, took care of her and made her dresses for very little reward. The Sphinx had a strong sense of the present which did not derive from a disdain of the past; it was never an effort for her to see a new point of view; in fact she welcomed change, was refreshed by the young by reason of the novelty of their tastes and thought. Those who have the attribute loosely called 'going with the times' do not merely bow with grace to the inevitable – the development of one idea from another; they know that this is a law of Nature to be accepted with adventurous excitement. In this way the Sphinx welcomed new inventions and different art forms. The slang of the

moment fascinated her, and so good was her literary ear that
she never made use of it in conversation if it was in the
slightest degree out-of-date.

The Sphinx made her home at the Washington Hotel in
Curzon Street after her daughter's marriage. As it was near
Trumper's, where Osbert Sitwell and many of his friends
had their hair cut, they would frequently drop in to tea or to
luncheon with her afterwards. They would find the small
figure of the Sphinx, dressed in black, waiting for them in
the lounge ready to discuss the latest gossip and news of the
literary, social, theatrical and artistic worlds. Ronald Firbank
would call at the Washington as he had in Florence, and
Peter Quennell, then a very young poet, would be brought
sometimes by the Sitwells. Once when he called alone he
found her with a sprained ankle. Her explanation for the
accident struck him as strange and typical of her. There was,
she told him, a piano in one of the public rooms of the hotel;
on this the Sphinx would sometimes play late at night some
hackneyed piece of classical music slightly incorrectly and by
ear. This was a secret pleasure to her. On one particular
evening she was playing the piano when she heard a movement behind a screen in the room. Horrified at being caught
by anyone playing such trash, she hurried away, and in
doing so slipped on the step of the dais on which the piano
stood.

A disadvantage of living at an hotel and travelling much
abroad was that the Sphinx could no longer keep a cat as a
pet. These animals she always adored, particularly if they
were black. One of her superstitions was that black cats
were lucky, as well as being beautiful; another, that seeing
the new moon through glass was unlucky. She and Osbert
would exchange warning telegrams or telephone calls at
appropriate and dangerous times. Excepting for visits to the
Sitwells at Renishaw and to her daughter in Wiltshire, the

Sphinx could rarely be induced to leave London, except for Italy. Her grandsons clamoured for her company; she had not lost the gift for entertaining children and did not believe in the theory that they should be treated kindly but firmly. This meant, in her opinion, that one gave them kindly everything they asked for, and when they became insupportable one firmly sent them away. Her system was better than that. It included reading *Alice in Wonderland* to them, which she enjoyed as much as they did.

Although the Sphinx belonged to the decadent movement of the Nineties, of which her two stories in *The Yellow Book* are an expression, it is interesting that there should be no touch of what is thought of as decadence in her novels; that is, if we accept Arthur Symons's definition of decadence as being 'an intense self-consciousness, a restless curiosity, an over-subtilizing refinement upon refinement, a spiritual and moral perversity'. In them she sometimes reveals that rare gift seen in its perfection in all the works of Max Beerbohm and in Wilde's best plays, of writing with a light touch, without triviality or facetiousness.

In 1933, while enjoying herself in Florence, the Sphinx became ill. When she returned to England pneumonia developed and caused her death. She was visited by those she loved until she was too ill to recognise them.

What was the Sphinx's secret? The solution may lie in her novels. Does not Colin MacInnes reveal it in these words? 'Although as a writer she is apparently uninvolved, in tone urbane, she really holds humane and moral views that determine a whole vision.' Osbert Sitwell suggests another in the following miniature portrait he gave to her:

> *O, Gilded Sphinx,*
> *Part prophetess, and part conspirator,*
> *Swirling your seven cloaks around you,*
> *What do you plot?*

To restore the rule of Isis, Ibis
And the Sacred Cat?
No, I will tell your secret!

Great loyalty, great wit:
   (Each strives against the other)
Both win: both lose; both benefit
In laughter none can smother.

Essential wisdom shows.
Alone, you know it is not silly
To scent the tuberose
And gild the lily.

Reminiscences, by Ada Leverson

(From *Letters to the Sphinx from Oscar Wilde* published in a limited edition by Duckworth in 1930.)

1. *The Importance of Being Oscar*

In the middle 'nineties, wealth, though not so rare as it is now, was already becoming scarce; there was even some fear that money might entirely vanish from the earth; and when two capitalists were heard one June night singing in a wood near Esher, Oscar Wilde wrote to *The Times* about it immediately. Money was spoken of in undertones and in offices; it was desired and valued as it is now, although 'prices' were not a regular conventional subject of conversation.

There was more margin; margin in every sense was in demand, and I remember, looking at the poems of John Gray (then considered the incomparable poet of the age), when I saw the tiniest rivulet of text meandering through the very largest meadow of margin, I suggested to Oscar Wilde that he should go a step further than these minor poets; that he should publish a book *all* margin; full of beautiful unwritten thoughts, and have this blank volume bound in some Nile-green skin powdered with gilt nenuphars and smoothed with hard ivory, decorated with gold by Ricketts (if not Shannon) and printed on Japanese paper; each volume must be a collector's piece, a numbered one of a limited 'first' (and last) edition: 'very rare'.

He approved.

'It shall be dedicated to you, and the unwritten text illustrated by Aubrey Beardsley. There must be five hundred signed copies for particular friends, six for the general public, and one for America.'

At this time, 1894 to 1895, London bloomed out into a sudden flamboyance of taste and of expression. Art, poetry, beauty, dress and decoration became the fashion; such subjects were talked about by everyone, however little most of them knew about it. If the Sheik had not yet been invented, 'chic' was greatly desired; phrases such as 'quite wonderful', 'simply perfect,' 'too lovely,' 'marvellous,' were the mode. Sentimental crises were discussed at great length and with leisurely enjoyment, with agonies of sympathy if unfortunate. The Overture to *Tannhäuser*, Daly's, the Gaiety, the Lyceum, *Mrs Tanqueray* were subjects of enthusiasm quite un-English; it is often, in fact, a Briton rather than a foreigner who 'gushes' while the Frenchman understates. Where an Englishman might say of a well-cooked dish that it was 'quite perfect' or 'excellent', the most a Frenchman would say would be 'Ca se mange'.

Where, in those days, was the strong silent man? Nowhere! Something weaker and more loquacious was required; and all these exuberant modes were certainly inaugurated by the poet-wit-dramatist Oscar Wilde; who loved, and made fashionable, rich brocades, rose-coloured tented-ceilings, yellow satin, 'a consolation for all the miseries of life'; jewels, and lavish flowers; in reaction from the severity and restraint of Morris and Ford Madox Brown and the other pre-Raphaelites, and also from the little Noah's-ark figures and the Noah's archaism of the forgotten aesthetic 'eighties. No more green and yellow! All was purple and gold. The hero of *Patience*, the subject of so many jests, had now a serious following. It was perhaps unfortunate that followers were allowed. Like all disciples, they had a way of being more Royalist than the King, remaining Royalist, indeed, after he had resigned, continuing to exploit a mode when its originator had long tired of it.

By the time Art-coal-scuttles had reached Balham, people who, when first fired by the fervid words of the young Oscar, had thrown their mahogany into the streets, were looking out for red-and-white ivory chessman, wax-flowers under glass, little horse-hair sofas and 'lustres,' desiring to have one perfect middle-Victorian room. The contrast in taste between the poet and his illustrator, Aubrey Beardsley, was very marked. Oscar loved purple and gold, Aubrey put everything down in black and white. And while every connoisseur declared the line of the young artist superb, there were others who deplored that he did not know where to draw it.

Life seemed very gay and easy then, and in superficial ways very much like the present time. The de Rezskes were singing, Lady de Grey encouraging music; Teddy Payne and Arthur Roberts amused us; and hadn't we Whistler, that great correspondent, always writing witty, insulting letters to people, publishing the letters at his own expense (and theirs), painting their portraits and tearing the pictures up in a rage, and always quarrelling until the public became quite confused in the grey mist as to which of the pictures was 'Battersea Bridge by Moonlight,' which 'Carlyle,' and which the 'Portrait of the Artist's Mother'?

The Apes-of-God (not long ago invented by Mr Wyndham Lewis but then known as the Hounds of Heaven) felt it their duty, or made it their business, to 'burn with a hard gem-like flame' (Pater's orders), to 'shrink from no experience,' to 'seek sensations'. This emotional self-expression resulted in the fashion, in the 'nineties, of frequent letters. Long, witty, sentimental letters (sent by private hansom cab, waiting-for-an-answer); passionate, long reply-paid telegrams; while the call of the district-messenger boy resounded in every home.

As Oscar Wilde himself once remarked, one can't go about abusing Heliogabalus, censuring Caesar Borgia, or scolding Nero. These figures have passed into the sphere of Art. So has our spectacular genius, Oscar Wilde. But the essential difference is that he was a man incapable of being either cruel or hard. The fault was weakness, and, with all his brilliance, a fatal want of judgment. Yet he is like them because he has become a legend. He was always a legend. He always will be.

Quicker in repartee and conversation than in his writing, he constantly made use in his work, afterwards, of things he had improvised.

I remember a serious young man, who, with others, was waiting his turn to speak to Oscar, asking him questions. The poet used several of these replies in his book *Intentions*.

'Will you very kindly tell me, Mr Wilde, in your own words, your viewpoint of George Meredith?'

'George Meredith is a prose Browning, and so is Browning.'

'Thank you. His style?'

'Chaos, illuminated by flashes of lightning.'

'And what do you think of Verlaine?'

'Verlaine is in the gutter, but he writes poetry on the pavement.'

'And Rudyard Kipling?'

'Ah! He has found that great thing for success, a new background. All palm trees, salaams and whisky-and-soda. His jaded Anglo-Indians show up on a superb background of vulgarity. He has seen some marvellous things through key-holes, has dropped more h's in his verse than any living man; *The Silver Man* is a masterpiece.'

Another man here came up, interrupting and slapping the poet on the shoulder, exclaiming 'Hullo, Oscar!'

Oscar looked up. He saw a stranger to him. He said, 'I don't know you by sight, but your manner is familiar.'

He told me that evening that a woman had come to him saying she had some screens sent from Japan, and asked him to advise her how to arrange them. 'Don't arrange them. Let them occur.'

A certain very kind and hospitable lady frequently invited Oscar to lunch and dine when he was at Dieppe after his

troubles. She was rather proud of her housekeeping econo-
mies, and mentioned that by buying a quantity at a time she
paid very little for her wine.

'How much do you think it costs?' she asked.

'I have no idea,' said Oscar, tasting it.

'Only about ninepence a bottle!' she replied.

He drank no more and put it down.

'Dreadful! It's curious; too bad, but wine-merchants always
cheat women disgracefully!' murmured Oscar.

2. The Last First Night

On Valentine's day. the 14th February, 1895, there was a
snow-storm more severe than had been remembered in
London for years. A black, bitter, threatening wind blew
the drifting snow. On that dark sinister winter's night,
when the first representation of *The Importance of Being
Earnest* was produced at the St James's Theatre, it was with
difficulty that one drove there at all, one had to go very
slowly on account of the horses. Crowds of hansoms,
broughams, carriages of all kinds blocked little King Street.

When at last we took refuge in the playhouse, how grateful
was the contrast! Outside, a frost, inside, the very breath of
success; perfumed atmosphere of gaiety, fashion and,
apparently, everlasting popularity. The author of the play was
fertile, inventive, brilliant; and with such encouragement
how could one realise that the gaiety was not to last, that
his life was to become dark, cold, sinister as the atmosphere
outside? Perfumed; for had not the word gone forth from
Oscar that the lily-of-the-valley was to be the flower of the
evening, as a souvenir of an absent friend? Flowers meant
much in those days, and nearly all the pretty women wore
sprays of lilies against their large puffed sleeves, while
rows and rows of young elegants had buttonholes of the
delicate bloom of lilies-of-the-valley. Most of the smart

young men held tall canes of ebony with ivory tops; they
wore white gloves with rows of black stitching and very
pointed shoes.

It was a distinguished audience, such as is rarely seen
nowadays, either at the Opera or even at a first night of a
Russian Ballet. The street just outside was crowded, not
only with the conveyances and the usual crowd of waiting
people, but with other Wilde fanatics who appeared to
regard the arrivals as part of the performance. Many of
these shouted and cheered the best-known people, and the
loudest cheers were for the author, who was as well known
as the Bank of England, as he got out of his carriage with
his pretty wife, who afterwards joined friends when the
author himself went behind the scenes.

What a rippling, glittering, chattering crowd was that!
They were certain of some amusement, for if, by exception,
they did not care for the play, was not Oscar himself sure to
do something to amuse them? Would he perhaps walk on
after the play smoking a cigarette, with a green carnation
blooming savagely in his coat, and saying, in his slow way,
with a slight smile (emphasizing certain words in the tradi-
tion of Swinburne), 'The *play* is de*light*ful, I've enjoyed myself *so* much?' Or, as on another occasion, would he bow
from a box and state in clear tones, heard all over the theatre,
that Mr Wilde was not in the house?

If he played to the Gallery, he got the Stalls.

There had been rumours for weeks that at Worthing Oscar
was writing a farce, and how each day he wrote a part of it and
each evening he read it to the Elect – his wife, children and a
few friends. He himself said it was a delicate bubble of fancy,
but in truth he cared little for any of his plays excepting only
Salome.

Influenced as he had been at the time by Maeterlinck,
Flaubert and Huysmans, yet *Salome* expressed *himself* in his

innate love of the gorgeous and the bizarre. (He said it was indeed unique: for it was written by an Irishman in French and done into English by a young Scottish friend!)

But to return to his first night – to be the last—

For months before, Lewis Waller had been tender and manly as The Ideal Husband, Sir George Alexander superb as Lord Windermere, and Beerbohm Tree had been witty and amusing in the favourite *A Woman of No Importance*. Oscar was, therefore, no novice. But he had not as yet written a farce.

Everyone was repeating his *mots*. Society at the moment was enthusiastic about that rarest of human creatures, a celebrity with good manners.

It is difficult now to convey in words the strange popularity, the craze there was at this moment for the subject of my essay. 'To meet Mr Oscar Wilde' was put on the most exclusive of invitation cards, yet every omnibus conductor knew his latest jokes. If he were caviare to the general, he was gentleman's-relish to the particular. His greatest pleasure was to amuse the mob, to frighten the burgess and to fascinate the aristocrat.

With his extraordinary high spirits and love of fun, he appealed to the lower classes; his higher gifts enchanted the artistic and such of the great world as wanted to amuse themselves; and with the sincere artist he was most himself. But the lower middle-class never liked him, always distrusted him and disliked his success.

People as a rule do not object to a man deserving success; only to his getting it.

Whoever still lives who was present on that night will remember the continual ripple of laughter from the very first moment, the excitement, the strange almost hysterical joy with which was received this 'Trivial Comedy for Serious People.' In some ways it was almost childish fun.

For a long time Oscar had been criticised for his continual use of paradox and epigram, witty, apt and cynical as they were, and the fashion of that period. At times they were considered wearying in the other plays. But how much sense there was in them really.

'Men marry because they are tired, women because they are curious.'

'The cynic is a person who knows the price of everything and the value of nothing.'

'The good American goes to Paris when he dies. Where do the bad Americans go? They go to America.'

Oscar's style of wit lent itself only too dangerously to imitation, and for years we suffered from a plethora of half-witted epigrams and feeble paradoxes by the mimics of his manner.

He had resolved to have nothing of this formula of wit in the farce. There was even a rollicking pun in the title. He intended it should be all Pure Nonsense. There is not a *mot*, not a paradox in the play, but the unexpectedness of this method pleased all the more, and when the curtain went down after the first act (which seemed to be principally about cucumber sandwiches) on the pathetic wail so well uttered by Allan Aynesworth, the childlike simplicity of the phrase 'But I haven't quite finished my tea!' was a triumph. Oscar had been right. When a friend said that the farce should be like a piece of mosaic, he answered, 'No; it must go like a pistol shot'.

And how they laughed when dignified George Alexander arrived on the stage in the deepest mourning, for the imaginary funeral of the fictitious Bunbury, who had now become a nuisance to his creator and had to die! (Black-tipped cigarettes were even suggested, but Alexander drew the line there.)

After the next act Oscar came to my box in which were the Beardsleys, Mabel and Aubrey, and other friends.

Before I first met Oscar, several years earlier, I had been told that he was rather like a giant with the wings of a Brazilian butterfly and I was not disappointed. But I thought him far more like a Roman Emperor who should have lived at the Pavilion at Brighton with George IV.

He was on this evening at the zenith of his careless, genial career, beaming and filled with that *euphoria* that was curiously characteristic of him when he was not in actual grief or pain. He had a low wide brow, with straight heavy hair into which the iron had entered, thus giving him the look of a Roman bust. His face was a clear red-brown from a long stay by the sea. He had blue-grey eyes and a well-formed mouth curved by a perpetual smile, and often a laugh of sincere humorous enjoyment of life. He had a superb vitality, a short-sighted joy in living for the moment. All genius has its naïf side, and he, a spectacular genius, greater, perhaps, as an improviser in conversation than as a writer, had this naïveté in excess. But I am not here intending to criticise either the work or the man; merely to give an impression of a period, and of one evening that has remained in my memory.

Oscar bore no trace, in 1895, of the pale slender long-haired youth who had met Sarah Bernhardt on her first arrival in England, his arms full of Madonna lilies, and had introduced the 'New Helen,' the Jersey Lily, the beautiful Mrs Langtry, to Millais, who painted her portrait and introduced her to Royalty. Oscar had written reams of verse to her and was so much in love with her that he insisted on lying on her doorstep half the night, and in the snow, too, until Mr Langtry, that legendary but yet, it seems, real figure, stumbled over him on returning from the club.

The poet was not now 'alone and palely loitering', like the victim of *La Belle Dame sans Merci*, 'the lady without a thank you', as the child translated it when the picture was hung in the Academy.

I can see Oscar now as he looked on the 14th February, 1895. He was dressed with elaborate dandyism and a sort of florid sobriety. His coat had a black velvet collar. He held white gloves in his small pointed hands. On one finger he wore a large scarab ring. A green carnation, echo in colour of the ring, bloomed in his buttonhole, and a large bunch of seals on a black moiré ribbon watch-chain hung from his white waistcoat. This costume, which on another man might have appeared perilously like fancy dress, and on his imitators was nothing less, seemed to suit him perfectly; he seemed at ease and to have the look of the last gentleman in Europe.

'Don't sit on the same chair as Aubrey. It's not compromising,' was his first remark. Aubrey Beardsley had a habit of folding up his long lank figure and perching on the arms of chairs. He had a quaint fund of rather sardonic humour, and was also a great dandy. He declared that he had caught a bad cold by leaving the tassel off his cane.

'What a contrast the two are,' Oscar continued, 'Mabel a daisy, Aubrey the most monstrous of orchids'.

The piece went splendidly, and we went after to supper at Willis's, a small restaurant then the fashion, famed for its cooking, its scarlet-leather seats and yellow candle-shades, only a few doors from the theatre. And as we walked there in the mud and blinding sleet, what a shock, what a horrible contrast to the warmth, the perfume within! Oscar did not join us at supper as he usually did. Some dark forecast perhaps – some chill presentiment; or perhaps because of the strange behaviour of the Marquess of Queensberry, who had left at the box-office an extraordinary bouquet of carrots, cauliflowers, turnips and other vegetables. It was already known that Oscar had bitter enemies as well as a

large crowd of friends. And if his chief enemy was eccentric,
many of his jealous rivals were quite unscrupulous.

It was a freezing cold night, and a black bitter wind blew on
Valentine's Day, the 14th February, 1895, that date of the
last first night.

3. *Afterwards*

The disagreement of the jury after the first trial left
Oscar, after his agonising ordeal, free for the time. But all
the hotels, clubs and even a large number of private friends
who had been almost fighting with each other a few weeks,
even days, ago to flatter and make much of him now refused
point-blank to receive him at all. He was like a hunted stag,
with no place to find refuge. He could not even take a room
at an hotel.

And this was not that the hotels, clubs and private friends
condemned him in any way at present. The question was in
abeyance, everything entirely depending on what the result
of the next trial might be. From place to place he went,
refused everywhere, with extreme politeness certainly,
for he might at any moment be re-installed and be the hero,
martyr and lion of the day. But they would not take the risk.

I do not mean that he had not many loyal and devoted
friends. But these were not in a position to offer him
hospitality.

He seemed so unhappy with his family at this time that
we asked him to stay with us, feeling that he would be more
at ease with friends than with relatives. Before he came, we
called all the servants together, parlour-maid, housemaid,
cook, kitchen-maid and our old nurse, Mrs Field, who acted
as my maid. We told them who was coming, offering them
a month's wages if they wished to leave at once. For the
affair was now such a scandal as had rarely been known.
Little else was talked of in London; the papers were full of

it; America, Germany, all the Continent joined in the
controversy, the foreigners saying, 'This is how you behave
to your poets,' while the Americans said, 'This is how your
poets behave'. Each servant in turn refused to leave. They
appeared proud to wait on 'poor Mr Wilde,' to whom
indeed they had been devoted ever since he had started
coming to the house. We sent the coachman away for a
holiday, as we feared he might talk in public-houses. The
others promised to keep the secret.

Then I went to fetch Oscar. He accepted with joy. And he
came back with me in the little pill-box brougham. When we
arrived I showed him his rooms, the nursery floor, which
was almost a flat in itself, two big rooms, one small one, and a
bathroom.

I asked him if he would like me to take away the toys in the
room. 'Please leave them,' he said. So in the presence of a
rocking-horse, golliwogs, a blue and white nursery dado
with rabbits and other animals on it, the most serious and
tragic matters were discussed. The poet leant his elbow on
the American cloth of the nursery table, and talked over the
coming trial with his solicitor.

While all our friends as well as the whole public were
discussing Oscar, no one had any idea that he was under our
roof.

He made certain rules in order to avoid any embarrassment
for us. He never left the nursery floor till six o'clock. He had
breakfast, luncheon and tea up there, and received all his
loyal friends there. He never would discuss his troubles
before me; such exaggerated delicacy seems today almost
incredible. But every day at six he would come down
dressed for dinner, and talk to me for a couple of hours in
the drawing-room. As always he was most carefully dressed,
there was a flower in his buttonhole, and he had received his
usual daily visit from the old hairdresser who shaved him

and waved his hair. His ambition was always to look like a Roman bust.

The old nurse, who waited on him, simply adored him. She always said, 'I never believe a word against Mr Wilde. He's a gentleman, if ever there was one.' Beerbohm Tree agreed with her: 'He remained *grand seigneur* to the last.'

When we were alone, he would walk up and down the room, always smoking a cigarette, talking in the most enchanting way about everything except his trouble.

Sometimes he would improvise prose poems, like those published in his works. Once he asked for writing things, to note one of these improvisations. I could not find any. 'You have all the equipment of a writer, my dear Sphinx, except pens, ink and paper.'

One day he was talking of the effect of absinthe. 'After the first glass, you see things as you wish they were. After the second, you see them as they are not. Finally you see things as they really are, and that is the most horrible thing in the world.'

'How do you mean?'

'I mean disassociated. Take a top-hat! You think you see it as it really is. But you don't, because you associate it with other things and ideas. If you had never heard of one before, suddenly saw it alone, you'ld be frightened, or laugh. That is the effect absinthe has, and that is why it drives men mad.'

He went on. 'Three nights I sat up all night drinking absinthe, and thinking that I was singularly clear-headed and sane. The waiter came in and began watering the sawdust. The most wonderful flowers, tulips, lilies and roses sprang up and made a garden of the *café*. "Don't you see them?" I said to him. "Mais non, Monsieur; il n'y a rien." '

He was also very romantic about opium and other drugs. He could not take them himself, they made him prosaically ill. Oscar loved to talk of the frequenters of the opium-dens in Limehouse. 'Who knows in what strange heaven they are suffering, what dull hells are teaching them the secret of some new joy?' He was the least neurotic man imaginable, and though Baudelaire and Poe appealed enormously to his imagination, he was utterly unlike them. He so much enjoyed everything, a joke, a sunset, talking to a child, that it was unnecessary for him, one felt, to 'chercher midi à quatorze heures.'

After dinner I would leave him with his friends; it was the only time of the day that they made serious plans, or, in fact, talked sense.

Generally he was extremely optimistic, firmly believing in a palmist's prophecy of triumph. One day his wife came to see him. They were alone for two hours.

I loved her very much, and was grieved to see her leave in tears. I found afterwards that she had come with an urgent message from her lawyer imploring him to go away without fail before the next trial, which would undoubtedly be his ruin.

Then came a look of immovable obstinacy on to his face. Nothing on earth would induce him to leave, though he knew that every facility was given to him. His mother told him it would be dishonourable for him to leave. Moreover, he never expected anything in his life to turn out badly.

Frank Harris tells the story of the yacht he had been lent to do what he liked with, and which was waiting to take the poet away. One evening he came to propose this to the poet, and asked me if I could row. Of course I said 'yes,' and saw myself as a fine ferryman. But Oscar absolutely refused.

The only time I ever suggested his going, I sent him up a little note, begging him to do as his wife asked him. When he came down to dinner, he gave me back my note, saying,

'That is not like you, Sphinx'. And then he began to talk of books.

He never liked even the grotesque part of Dickens. To those who praised Dickens, he said, 'One must have a heart of stone to read the death of Little Nell without laughing'.

Of Max Beerbohm he said, 'He plays with words as one plays with what one loves'. Adding, 'When you are alone with him, Sphinx, does he take off his face and reveal his mask?'

The morning came when he was to leave for his ordeal. The night before he had asked me to put a sleeping-draught on his mantelpiece. He never intended to take it, but just the presence of it had, he said, a magical effect.

In the hall he suddenly turned to me and said, for the first time in a faltering voice, 'If the worst comes to the worst, Sphinx, you'll write to me?'

Then he and his friend, Mr Adey, left in the little pill-box brougham which I had hired for him.

Later in the same day I received a telegram to tell me what had happened. I did not see him again for two years.

When Oscar was again a free man, he found himself without his mother and his brother, who both had died, and without his children – for whom a guardian had been appointed. But he felt most of all the death of his wife. She came to see him very frequently during the two years; always she was kind and devoted. Then she was ill, and died at Genoa after an operation.

This was the greatest blow to Oscar. As soon as possible he went to Genoa and visited her grave. He drove out to it in a little ramshackle fly, a green one. He abandoned himself to a passion of grief, repentance and bitter remorse; and amid the lavish crimson roses with which he covered the grave, he broke down, sobbed and prayed, and made vows of eternal fidelity to her memory. He had been very sincerely in love with her, and he felt now that only some madness had made him cause her sorrow. He was shattered and broken after this violent emotion, and shed tears in the fly as he was driven away.

In his curious temperament there were many contradic- tions. Suddenly his sadness left him. He became peculiarly gay and almost reckless. And it was several days before he thought to dismiss the cab.

Oscar once told a friend of a strange experience that he never forgot and later often thought of.

When first married, he was quite madly in love, and showed himself an unusually devoted husband. He never left his wife for an hour, and she adored him in return. A few months after their marriage, she went shopping, and Oscar accompanied her. He waited for her outside Swan and Edgar's while she made some long and tedious purchases.

As he stood there full of careless good spirits, on a cold sunny May morning, a curious, very young, but hard-eyed creature appeared, looked at him, gave a sort of laugh, and passed on. He felt, he said, 'as if an icy hand had clutched his heart'. He had a sudden presentiment. He saw a vision of folly, misery and ruin. And remained in a depressed state for the rest of the evening.

Very early one very cold May morning my husband, I, and several other friends drove from our house in Deanery Street to meet Oscar at the house in Bloomsbury of the Rev. Stuart Headlam. The drawing-room was full of Burne- Jones and Rossetti pictures, Morris wall-paper and curtains, in fact an example of the decoration of the early 'eighties, very beautiful in its way, and very like the aesthetic rooms Oscar had once loved.

We all felt intensely nervous and embarrassed. We had the English fear of showing our feelings, and at the same time the human fear of not showing our feelings.

He came in, and at once he put us at our ease. He came in with the dignity of a king returning from exile. He came in talking, laughing, smoking a cigarette, with waved hair and a flower in his button-hole, and he looked markedly better, slighter, and younger than he had two years previously. His first words were, 'Sphinx, how marvellous of you to know exactly the right hat to wear at seven o'clock in the morning to meet a friend who has been away! You can't have got up, you must have sat up.' He talked on lightly for some time, then wrote a letter, and sent it in a cab to a Roman Catholic Retreat, asking if he might retire there for six months. While waiting, he walked up and down, and said: 'The dear Governor, such a delightful man, and his wife is charming. I spent happy hours in their garden, and they asked me to spend the summer with them. They thought I was the gardener.' He began to laugh. 'Unusual, I think? but I don't feel I can. I feel I want a change of scene.'

'Do you know one of the punishments that happen to people who have been "away"? They are not allowed to read *The Daily Chronicle!* Coming along I begged to be allowed to read it in the train. "No!" Then I suggested I might be allowed to read it upside down. This they consented to allow, and I read all the way *The Daily Chronicle* upside down, and never enjoyed it so much. It's really the only way to read newspapers.'

The man returned with the letter. We all looked away while Oscar read it. They replied that they could not accept him in the Retreat at his impulse of the moment. It must be thought over for at least a year. In fact they refused him.

Then he broke down and sobbed bitterly. I left, and heard later that he went to Berneval with friends. Oscar had a wonderful power of recuperation, and soon recovered his spirits.

Later I went to Paris to see him, and found him at that

time leading the life of a student in a tiny room at the Hôtel
d'Alsace. He was unique in his power of making people fond
of him. It is known that his landlord lent him hundreds of
pounds.

In this sketch, for it is no more, I am making no attempt
to criticise or appraise either the man or his work. I speak
solely of what was in my personal knowledge.

Oscar was the most generous man I have ever met, and he
showed his kindness always in the most graceful way.

A young solicitor whom he knew only slightly, told him
that he was madly in love with a marvellously lovely girl of
sixteen. She had red hair, violet eyes, and black eyelashes,
and had a great likeness to the portraits of Rossetti's
wife and the wife of William Morris. Her name was
Marjorie.

'How much would you actually need in order to marry
Marjorie?' asked Oscar.

'A hundred and fifty pounds. Then I could take a tiny
flat and work. She is earning her own living.'

Oscar had just received a large sum for *Lady Windermere's
Fan*. He wrote a cheque that moment for a hundred and sixty
pounds, and gave it to the young man, saying peremptorily,
'Go *at once*, and marry her, boy, and bring her to our house
at Worthing for your honeymoon'.

He did so, and Oscar was worshipped by them both ever
afterwards. Marjorie was the other woman who went to
meet him after he had been 'away'. She was quite as incredibly
lovely as the young man had said, and very sweet and clever.

He had many devoted friends, who remained always loyal
to him. Chief among these was Robert Ross. There was
indeed no trouble he would not take to advance a friend's
interest, and I think he rather resented any friend who was
not in actual need of help. *A propos* of this, Oscar Wilde
once improvised a fable in the style of the Lives of the Saints.

He called it Saint Robert of Phillimore. (It was in Phillimore Gardens that Robbie's people lived.)

Saint Robert of Phillimore

There was a certain Saint, who was called Saint Robert of Phillimore. Every night, while the sky was yet black, he would rise from his bed and, falling on his knees, pray to God that He, of His great bounty, would cause the sun to rise and make bright the earth. And always, when the sun rose, Saint Robert knelt again and thanked God that this miracle had been vouchsafed. Now, one night, Saint Robert, wearied by the vast number of more than usually good deeds that he had done that day, slept so soundly that when he awoke the sun had already risen, and the earth was already bright. For a few moments Saint Robert looked grave and troubled, but presently he fell down on his knees and thanked God that, despite the neglectfulness of His servant, He had yet caused the sun to rise and make bright the earth.

One of the hits in *The Importance of Being Earnest* is when the clergyman says that Mr Bunbury expressed a desire to be buried in Paris. 'I fear,' says the clergyman, 'that this doesn't seem a very desirable state of mind at the last'.

Oscar is buried in Paris under Epstein's magnificent monument given, ten years after his death, by a lady whose friendship remained steadfast to the end.*

---

* Mrs Carew, the mother of Sir Coleridge Kennard.

INDEX

124